**The Orientalist Museum**

presents the exhibition

# *Heritage of Art Diplomacy*
## Memoirs of an Ambassador

يقدم متحف المستشرقين معرض

# موروث دبلوماسية الفن
## مذكرات سفير

On display at the Museum of Islamic Art
in the 4th floor galleries
from January 25 - March 18, 2013

في قاعات العرض في الطابق الرابع في متحف الفن الإسلامي
من ٢٥ يناير ولغاية ١٨ مارس ٢٠١٣

موروث دبلوماسية الفن
مذكرات سفير
Heritage of Art Diplomacy
Memoirs of an Ambassador

# CONTENTS

# FOREWORD

## Dr Oliver Watson
## Director, Museum of Islamic Art
## Doha – Qatar

The opening of the Museum of Islamic Art in Doha, Qatar, in the autumn of 2008 is an important event on many levels and from many aspects: the opening to the public of an extraordinary collection of Islamic art, housed in a building of global architectural importance, in a country at the heart of the Islamic world.

It is the realization of a vision promoted for nearly two decades by HH Sheikh Hamad bin Khalifa Al Thani, Emir of the State of Qatar. It stands as one of the main foundations of his ambition to make Qatar a regional and international centre for culture and education. The Museum of Islamic Art is but the first of a series of museums and institutions which will cover all the interests and aspirations of human kind – a project being energetically taken forward under the leadership of HE Sheikha al Mayassa bint Hamad bin Khalifa Al Thani, Chairperson of the Qatar Museums Authority.

The Museum of Islamic Art is naturally focused on the artistic achievements of the Islamic world. This is something that is of enormous educational importance at the present time. Important in providing the citizens of Qatar with a key means by which to appreciate and understand their rightful legacy – not simply a national legacy but as inheritors of an international culture. Important in showing Muslims worldwide the historic global connections of the Islamic lands and, through art, the excellence and pre-eminence of their intellectual and economic life. And, in particular for non-Muslims throughout the world today, important in demonstrating how Islam has continually been a tolerant and progressive force, adopting, adapting and passing on ideas within and across its borders.

These things are particularly well illustrated by the history of art – a history that over the centuries has shown a continual renewal, an eager interest in new ideas and a great sophistication and accomplishment in production. Islamic art is in part devoted to the promotion and expression of the religion of Islam, but much is also concerned with secular and domestic life. Even the artistic expression of non-Muslim communities within the Islamic world partakes of an aesthetic that is part of Islamic culture.

The Museum of Islamic Art is housed in a landmark building by the Chinese-American architect I. M. Pei. Unlikely as it may at first seem, this building embodies many essential elements of Islamic architecture – in particular the interest in the way light articulates space. It provides a fitting setting for the display of an internationally important collection.

The collections of the Museum are by any measure extraordinary, especially impressive as they have been gathered together in a very short time. They are not large in number by comparison with other major museums, but of a quality and breadth of interest quite the equal of any collection anywhere. They range geographically over thousands of kilometres, from Spain to Central Asia and India, and in time over a thousand years, from the seventh to the nineteenth century. Every area has pieces of the utmost quality, and some sections – carpets, inlaid metalwork and early calligraphy, for example – are among the most impressive and important to be found anywhere.

This small book seeks to provide visitors with a guide and souvenir, and to encourage those who have not yet visited to do so. The quality of the building and the collections provide all the justification needed.

# THE ARCHITECTURE

## The Architectural Design of the Doha Museum of Islamic Art

The Museum of Islamic Art stands in Doha on an artificial island at the beginning of the Corniche, its faceted exterior planes orchestrating brilliant sun and dark shadows. One of the final works of the architect I. M. Pei, this building speaks of modern architecture, but also of the essence of Islam. Within, visitors will find one of the most sophisticated and advanced museum presentations in the world, the work of the noted French designer Jean-Michel Wilmotte. Bringing these two important figures of modern architecture together is an important gesture, one that speaks of the long history and culture of Islam as much as it does of the rise of shining new cities on the shores of the Arabian Gulf. Culture is what nurtured civilization here, beginning centuries ago. When they venture onto the island where the Museum of Islamic Art stands, the citizens of Qatar and neighbouring states, together with visitors from around the world, will find a bridge that crosses the centuries, linking the material culture of Islam to the art, architecture and design of today.

## I. M. Pei. The Journey to Doha

The journey in time and space of I. M. Pei from his native China to Doha is of significance not only for the success and relevance of the Museum itself, but also for contemporary architecture in general. Where modern architecture often sought to make a clean break with the past, in the works he has designed since becoming engaged in the Grand Louvre project in Paris (1983–93), Pei has looked deeply into the culture of cities and countries where he has built, from Luxembourg to Suzhou in China, where his family lived for 600 years, and on to the hills of Shigaraki near Kyoto, where he built the Miho Museum. Remaining faithful to his modern ideal, and still seeking to bring forth the essence of a culture, I. M. Pei has in many ways redefined what it means to be modern. In his work, the break with the past or tabula rasa exemplified by Le Corbusier's Plan Voisin (1925), which sought to demolish much of central Paris in favour of a new city, has effectively been healed. There never was any question in Pei's work of superficial references to history such as those briefly rendered popular by the Post-Modern movement

in architecture; rather, in Doha and elsewhere, he has sought and found the real cultural links that inevitably should bring the past, present and future together.

Born in China in 1917, I. M. Pei moved to the United States to study architecture at the age of eighteen, obtaining his degrees at the Massachusetts Institute of Technology (MIT, Bachelor in Architecture, 1940) and at the Harvard Graduate School of Design (Master's in Architecture 1946), when Modernism in architecture was at its height. Both at Harvard under the aegis of Walter Gropius and at the Illinois Institute of Technology where Ludwig Mies van der Rohe held sway, Modernism, as it developed in America, frequently sought to sweep aside the past in favour of a bright new future. It was a reaction that originated in European politics, but was more easily accepted in the United States, where history holds a different place than it might in Paris or Moscow. From a country that embraces the new, Pei moved, after 1988, to the older societies of Europe and Asia, where history is a deeper current defining identity. This is the intellectual background of I. M. Pei's emergence as an architect, one that he has progressively moulded according to his own vision. Architecture critics tend to have a specific vision of their own country, and may readily defend one school or another. Viewing the work of I. M. Pei requires a broader vision, one that admits that true modernity need not reject the past, and may well embrace different cultures.

Winner of the 1983 Pritzker Prize and of the 1989 Praemium Imperiale, I. M. Pei has been recognized as one of the leading architects of our time. And yet, to understand the importance of his contribution, it is necessary

PRECEDING PAGES The monumental entrance sequence of the Museum features a double row of palm trees and a central water course that animates the drive.

"THIS WAS ONE OF THE MOST DIFFICULT JOBS I EVER UNDERTOOK. IT SEEMED TO ME THAT I HAD TO GRASP THE ESSENCE OF ISLAMIC ARCHITECTURE." **I. M. PEI**

to do more than leaf through the pages of a book, looking at the spectacular images of his vaulting atriums and light-filled spaces. One must stand on the Mall in Washington, so close to the essence of American identity, and see how he has indelibly marked the Mall with the East Building of the National Gallery of Art, bringing the best of architecture and modern art alongside the seat of power. One must stand in the courtyard of the Louvre at nightfall and see how the Pyramid brings this focal point of French history to life, at the end of the axis of the Champs-Elysées. One must travel to Shigaraki in Japan to visit his remarkable Miho Museum, where architecture is at one with nature, art and the spirit of place. Few, if any, modern architects have ranged as broadly across the world or sought as actively to understand the cultures where they have built as I. M. Pei. No other architect has designed buildings in the heart of New York, Washington D.C., Paris and Suzhou, as well as in the hills of Shigaraki, and, today, on the tip of the Corniche in Doha.

## Mountains and Clouds

In Paris, Pei explains that the Pyramid resulted in part from his reflection on the work of the great French garden designer André Le Nôtre (1613–1700), who laid out the triumphal axis leading from the Louvre in the direction of the Champs-Elysées. It is no accident that the glass surface of the Pyramid reflects the Parisian sky, even as it defines the entrance area below, which is flooded with light. Despite the controversy that initially greeted I. M. Pei's proposal to place a pyramid in the courtyard of the Louvre, it has in many ways become a symbol of France since it opened in 1989. The Richelieu Wing of the Louvre, which long housed the Ministry of Finance, was reopened in 1993 for the bicentenary of the Louvre after Pei had transformed and finally integrated it into the greatest museum in the world. The fact that I. M. Pei succeeded in bringing the Louvre into the twentieth century is a measure of his capacity to understand the real meaning of the prestigious locations where he has had the privilege and responsibility to build.

In Suzhou, China, so close to his own family's history, I. M. Pei made reference to Chinese painting in the rockwork design he created in the new museum's courtyard. The city's gardens, part of the Unesco World Heritage list, are its most profound cultural expression. "Rocks became very important in gardens," explains I. M. Pei. "They are like sculptures. Poets and painters worked on rock gardens beginning in the Yuan Dynasty,[1] but they do not have painters and poets who do this anymore. I told my client, the mayor of Suzhou, that we did not have the painterly eyes necessary – the craftsmen for rocks. I wanted to try something else, something new. I sent a young man to Shandong Province (near Korea) where there are many rocks. They have huge boulders that can be cut with a steel wire: it was a silhouette I was looking for. Forty or fifty slices of rock came to Suzhou – which normally would cost a fortune, but not in China. I selected about thirty of them and then, in 2005, I went there and they were all on the ground, so I sat at a table in the middle of what is now the pond and looked at that wall. I had the reproduction of a painting by a great Song Dynasty artist in front of me, Mi Fei's Mountains and Clouds.[2] There was a crane there – so they put pieces up and down as I wished. I did that for about a week and finally got something that looked reasonably good. At least it is a way of using rock in Suzhou within the limited space

**RIGHT** Seen from the gardens to the right of the main entrance drive, the Museum takes on an increased complexity, with the strong form of the central dome standing out in front of the darker top of the main atrium window.

"IT IS THE LIGHT OF THE DESERT THAT TRANSFORMS THE ARCHITECTURE INTO A PLAY OF LIGHT AND SHADOW." **I. M. PEI**

we have. Have I done anything that will be useful for the future? I do not think so, but it is a way to get people to look. It is a sort of three-dimensional painting after the work of Mi Fei."[3]

As expressed in I. M. Pei's own words, be it in Paris, or Suzhou, it is clear that he has sought out the essence of cultures, the geometry and illusion of Le Nôtre, or the dream-like landscapes of Mi Fei. Going beyond architecture to garden design, literature and painting, Pei's quest is clear, but this is not the usual course of contemporary architecture. In this respect, due to the global span, particularly of his late career, he stands in a category apart. As the citation for the Pritzker Prize affirmed in 1983: "Ieoh Ming Pei has given this century some of its most beautiful interior spaces and exterior forms. Yet the significance of his work goes far beyond that. His concern has always been the surroundings in which his buildings rise."

## From West to East

The Pritzker Prize was in a sense a well-merited consecration of I. M. Pei's long career in America, and yet, even as he accepted that award, he was embarking on the second phase of his work, visiting Paris to understand just how the complex Louvre palace could be brought into the twentieth century and made coherent as a museum. Pei says today that the Louvre was a clear turning point in his life. As the design work in Paris drew to a close in 1988, he retired from the company he had created, Pei Cobb Freed & Partners, and set up his own small firm, I. M. Pei Architect, resolving to accept only projects that were of interest to him. "I was brought up in a certain way, architecturally speaking – it was not Chinese, it was American," he says today. "That is what makes it interesting for me to be exposed to different cultures. I selected places to work where I did not know the cultures. Every project I have taken

on since I stopped working in America has been a learning process."[4] It was thus that he worked successively on an extension of the German Historical Museum (Berlin, Germany, 1998–2003), the Miho Museum (Shigaraki, Shiga, Japan, 1998–2002), Mudam Luxembourg (Musée d'Art Moderne Grand-Duc Jean, Luxembourg, 1999–2006) and the more recent Suzhou Museum (Suzhou, China, 2003–06). In each case he sought the most significant elements of the sites and cultures involved to create buildings that, considered together, redefine the relationship between history and modernity laid down in good part by Europeans teaching in America in the wake of World War II.

The architect's involvement in Doha came subsequent to a 1997 competition that selected the Lebanese architect Rasem Badran. As I. M. Pei explains the situation: "Badran's project unfortunately did not go forward and I was

**ABOVE** An angular view of the Museum shows just how its facade planes come to life in the strong Doha sun, sharply dividing light and shadow.

contacted by Luis Monreal, who had been a member of the original jury. Mr Monreal, now General Manager of the Aga Khan Trust for Culture, knew that I did not participate in competitions, but he persuaded the Emir that I might be a good choice to design the new Museum. I was offered a number of sites along the Corniche, including the originally planned location, but I did not accept these options. There were not yet too many buildings nearby, but I feared that in the future large structures might rise up that would overshadow it. I asked if it might not be possible to create my own site. This was very selfish of me of course, but I knew that in Qatar it is not too complicated to create landfill."[5] He thus located the Museum of Islamic Art on the south side of the Corniche on a man-made island sixty metres from the shore. A new C-shaped peninsula provides protection from the Persian Gulf to the north and from industrial buildings to the east. As was the case for the Louvre, or indeed for the East Building of the National Gallery in Washington, Pei has benefited from a remarkable conjugation of circumstances and his own intuition to build on the most prestigious conceivable sites. In Doha, more by his own doing than in some previous projects, he again succeeded in positioning his building in a unique and significant way.

Once he had accepted the commission in Doha, it might be said that I. M. Pei went on a journey in time and space to discover his inspiration. "This was one of the most difficult jobs I ever undertook. It seemed to me that I had to grasp the essence of Islamic architecture. The difficulty of my task was that Islamic culture is so diverse, ranging from Iberia to Mughal India, to the gates of China and beyond. I was familiar with the Grand Mosque in Cordoba (784–766, 961–966, 987–990) and I thought that it represented the pinnacle of Islamic architecture, but I was wrong. The combined influence of climate and the culture of Spain meant that Cordoba was not the pure expression I was seeking. The same was true, for different reasons, of Fatehpur Sikri, a

Mughal capital where one of the largest mosques in India, the Jama Masjid, was built. I recognize that my intellectual process might be considered very subjective, but here the Indian influence is tangible, and, again, I did not find my inspiration. Even the Umayyad Great Mosque in Damascus (709–715), the oldest extant monumental mosque, seems to carry with it elements of the history of Rome or of early Christianity – a Roman temple and a Byzantine church had stood on this site before the mosque was built. Where Byzantine influence could be felt, I again decided that my quest had not reached its goal. I went to Tunisia and, although my intention had been to examine the mosques, I was taken with another type of architecture in the form of the ribat (fort) at Sousse (821). There I felt I was coming closer to the essence of Islamic architecture, where sunlight brings to life powerful volumes and geometry plays a central role."[6]

## The Essence of Islam

Returning with a visible passion to his quest for what he considers the "essence of Islamic architecture," I. M. Pei says: "I began to understand why I felt that Cordoba was not truly representative of the essence I was seeking. It is too lush and colourful. If one could find the heart of Islamic architecture, might it not lie in the desert, severe and simple in its design, where sunlight brings forms to life? I was finally coming closer to the truth, and I believe I found what I was looking for in the mosque of Ahmad Ibn Tulun in Cairo (876–879). The small ablutions fountain surrounded by double arcades on three sides, a slightly later addition to the architecture, is an almost Cubist expression of geometric progression from the octagon to the square and the square to the circle. It is no accident that Le Corbusier learned much from the architecture of the Mediterranean and the architecture of Islam. This severe architecture comes to life in the sun, with its shadows and shades of colour. I had

at last found what I came to consider to be the very essence of Islamic architecture in the middle of the mosque of Ibn Tulun." The relationship between the final form of the Doha Museum of Islamic Art and the high domed ablutions fountain (sabil) erected in the central courtyard of the Ibn Tulun Mosque in the thirteenth century is clear, even if the scale of the Pei building is much larger. Ibn Tulun, the oldest mosque in Cairo to have survived in its original form, is also the largest mosque in Cairo in terms of its site. Although the sources for its design are the focus of some debate amongst scholars, it is clear that Ibn Tulun is a truly significant example of early Muslim architecture. Embraced in its otherwise empty courtyard by the brown rising dust of

ABOVE The central courtyard of the mosque of Ahmad Ibn Tulun in Cairo (876879). The distinctive high domed sabil (ablutions fountain), seen on the right in this image, was added in the central courtyard in the late 13th century by the Mamluk Sultan Lajin.

ABOVE The arcades of the courtyard that separate the Education Wing from the Museum itself might bring to mind those of Ibn Tulun, seen on the previous double page. In the distance, the skyline of Doha.

"This severe architecture comes to life in the sun, with its shadows and shades of colour. I had at last found what I came to consider to be the very essence of Islamic architecture in the middle of the mosque of Ibn Tulun." **I. M. Pei**

modern Cairo, the central fountain of Ibn Tulun is a work of such purity and simplicity as to escape any classification. If its substance is ancient, its form is the result of geometric calculations, which forcibly lie at the heart of modern architecture. It is in the universal quality of its proportions that I. M. Pei resolved his quest for the 'essence' of Islam.

Pei's design for the Museum in Doha is intimately related to the architecture of Islam, but also, in an even more fundamental way, it has to do with the way the sun shines in these confines of the desert and the sea. "To understand Islamic architecture you have to go to Tunisia, for example," he says. "In Monastir, the birthplace of Habib Bourguiba, Tunisia's first president, there is a fort – the ribat of Harthema built in 796 by Harthema ibn Ayun, a huge place with serrated walls. It looked wonderful under the sun. Inside there are courtyards, a harem, with tiny little rooms. On the other side was the barracks for the soldiers. In the courtyard there is a huge tree. Without the sun you would not want to go in. The sun brings things to life. That impressed me."[7] With his atria and glazed walls, I. M. Pei has consistently incorporated the effects of the sun in his buildings, thus bringing them to life, but on the eastern edge of the Arabian Peninsula there could be no question of such ample window surfaces. The lessons of the past had to be observed and understood.

## From the Outside, In

The austerity of the exterior of the Doha Museum of Islamic Art contrasts with the use of decorative patterns and forms employed by Pei inside the building. Aside from the rather elaborate metal entrance canopy, the building is essentially planar. The same can, of course, be said of the East Building of the National Gallery in Washington, though larger glazed surfaces are in evidence there. Obviously without reference to Islam in Washington, Pei exploited the remarkable variety of shapes and light that can be derived from an assemblage of triangles. On the basis of a simple geometric form, he created a spatial complexity, heightened in the case of the National Gallery by bridges, tunnels and a central atrium, that announces a modernity that has gone beyond Modernism. "I remained faithful to the inspiration I had found in the mosque of Ibn Tulun, derived from its austerity and simplicity," he says. "It was this essence that I attempted to bring forth in the desert sun of Doha. It is the light of the desert that transforms the architecture into a play of light and shadow. My design has only one major window – it is forty-five-metres high and faces the Arabian Gulf. I must admit that I have allowed myself another subjective decision, which was based on my feeling that Islamic architecture often comes to life in an explosion of decorative elements, such as in the courtyard of the Umayyad Mosque in Damascus, or the interior of the Dome of the Rock in Jerusalem (687–691), for example. I have also particularly admired perforated metalwork in Egypt. The central space climaxes in the oculus of an ornate stainless-steel dome that captures patterned light in its multiple facets. A geometric matrix transforms the dome's descent from circle to octagon, to square, and finally to four triangular flaps that angle back at different heights to become the atrium's column supports." The visitor entering the Museum is almost immediately confronted with the surprising, sculptural double Grand Stair, designed specifically to allow a view toward the monumental window described by Pei. The third step up this stairway is precisely below the centre of the dome, while the floor below shows an intricate decorative pattern, inspired by the geometric interlaces of Islamic tradition, but still visibly modern. The dome, it is true, captures light in its facets, admitting shafts of sun that move across its surface, giving life and movement to the space below.

The main level houses temporary exhibition galleries, together with prayer halls for men and women, the museum shop, a 200-seat auditorium and a fountain café. The atrium space was designed by I. M. Pei, while the shop and exhibition galleries were the work of Jean-Michel Wilmotte, working within the forms created by Pei. The window, facing the burgeoning skyline of Doha's new towers, is protected from sun and dampens sound through the use of a screen of acoustical aluminium rods. Each level of the exhibition floors is spanned by glass bridges that pass above the fountain café, completing the circulation path of the U-shaped balconies cantilevered around the atrium. The transparency and sheer height of the bridges that cross over the atrium space can certainly be described as vertiginous. While daylight enters from the oculus of the dome and the great window, the overpasses give a somewhat Piranesian ambiance to the atrium, a complexity heightened by the decorative patterns and the sweeping double stair. A boat dock with large pierced metal lanterns, intended specifically for use by the Emir, is set at a 90° angle vis-à-vis the main entrance, and intentionally faces the Emiri Diwan, the governmental headquarters of the ruler of Qatar. Though the central dome of the Museum may bring to mind a certain number of mosque structures, the architect has not aligned his building, or its great window, in the direction of Mecca. The mihrab, a niche in the wall of a mosque that indicates the qibla (the direction that Muslims should face when praying), is rarely, if ever, designed as a window, but the elongated, axial form and position of the great window in the Museum does bring to mind this aspect of Islamic architecture. Prayer facilities within the Museum naturally take up the correct alignment, however, and are rotated slightly vis-à-vis the rest of the building.

With a building area of 35,500 square metres, this is not simply a place of display for a new collection of Islamic art. True to the original vision of the client, who saw it as a centre of culture and education in the State, the Museum

RIGHT Rectangles, triangles and an arc form the deceptively simple facade as seen from this angle, changing constantly as the sun moves through the sky.

includes an expansive Education Centre, reached by walking through a covered passageway that opens onto an arcaded garden with a fountain and central gazebo. This garden, perhaps best suited to the cooler months of the year (summer temperatures can reach over 50° C), has a spectacular view across the bay to the rising forest of towers that forms the new heart of Doha. The central gazebo undoubtedly bears some comparison to the tea pavilions designed in England (Oare Pavilion, Wiltshire, 1999–2003) and Suzhou by Pei. A thin, elegant bridge from the exterior also allows visitors to approach the Education Centre directly, without passing through the museum lobby.

The Museum of Islamic Art in Doha has taken on the ambitious task of altering visions of Islamic art. Long the province of non-Muslim Western curators and specialists, this institution is intended to show Islamic art where it was made in the figurative sense if not precisely in the literal one. Perhaps more austere than many of Pei's other buildings, this architecture is meant, like the central fountain of Ibn Tulun, to live in the desert light. Harsh and uncompromising, this light makes the forms and colours of the Museum change throughout the day, glowing orange in the setting sun. Inside the Museum, the objects emerge from the darkness, lit to underline a particular aspect or fact, to make them speak as it were, to bring forth their beauty.

I. M. Pei concludes his description of this project with a homage to the French interior designer Jean-Michel Wilmotte, who worked with him previously on the Louvre and again in Doha, principally in the exhibition gallery, bookshop and offices: "The interior will be the best ever. I recommended Wilmotte and the client went to see his work at the Louvre and decided he was good. In Doha, you can see an installation like nothing you have ever seen before. There are huge glass doors on the display cases that move at the touch of a button. They work perfectly. I am more than satisfied; I think it is incredible."[8] I. M. Pei provided the Museum with a series of geometrically arranged

"I HAVE ALLOWED MYSELF [A] SUBJECTIVE DECISION, WHICH WAS BASED ON MY FEELING THAT ISLAMIC ARCHITECTURE OFTEN COMES TO LIFE IN AN EXPLOSION OF DECORATIVE ELEMENTS..." **I. M. PEI**

galleries which were essentially 'black boxes' left to the skills of the designer to bring forth the stunning beauty of the collections of Islamic decorative arts. Wilmotte has played on a subtle range of dark, high-quality materials that stand back and allow the dramatically lit objects to take centre stage. The intentionally oversized display cases allow the works to appear to float in space, imposing their own scale on this vast Museum. Rather than putting his own contribution to the fore, Wilmotte appears to have deliberately allowed his display cases and galleries to cede to the objects they contain. If this approach seems logical, it is far from being current amongst designers intent on making their own reputation. With clients like the Louvre or the Rijksmuseum in Amsterdam, Wilmotte is surely no longer out to prove himself, and, indeed, his reputation from the first was based on an innate ability to bring objects and architectural forms to life in a subtle, intelligent way.

Jean-Michel Wilmotte has undoubtedly grasped the spirit and ideas of Pei's architecture and the juncture between the two men's work in Doha is seamless. I. M. Pei undertook a personal journey in search of the essence of Islam. What he found was undoubtedly 'personal', but to the extent that he was successful, this interpretation also tends to put forward what can only be described as the 'universal', or fundamentally human qualities inscribed in the art and history of Islam. The values that the collection seeks to bring forth in the art of Islam exist too in the austere planes and curves of the fountain of Ibn Tulun. To seek and to find the way that sunlight plays on these forms and to understand that this is the architecture of a region and a culture in its purest incarnation are the qualities that imbue Pei's architecture. Within, Islamic decorative patterns strike the heart and mind of I. M. Pei because from the first he was a man of modernity, of geometry applied to buildings in a way that makes them live. The triangular patterns that dominate the East

Building of the National Gallery in Washington, for example, have more to do with the shape of the site on the city's Mall, and yet there, too, geometry and light bring the architecture to life. The East Building has no relation to the architecture of Islam except in the profound sense that it is formed by geometry and light. In the final analysis the 'universal' becomes, the 'human'.

I. M. Pei is typically modest in discussing his own accomplishments in Doha, and it is true that opinions are divided as to the wisdom of attempting to distil the modern 'essence' of the architecture of such a vast domain as Islam. There are gestures seen here, such as the monumental round chandelier that hangs below the dome, undoubtedly akin to the great circular lighting fixtures seen in Ottoman mosques, that make the reference to Islam all but explicit. A large ring lamp hangs from the dome of the Süleymaniye Mosque in Istanbul (1550–57), for example. I. M. Pei remains circumspect about any relation of his interior design for the Doha Museum of Islamic Art to that of mosques, however, no matter where they might be. He refers rather to secular sources. "The Islamic decorative arts amazed me by their beauty," he says. "Ibn Tulun is rather harsh, but for the interior I went elsewhere for inspiration. When you have the sun, architecture does not need anything; all you need is the faceting and then you get all the richness you want. But people do not stay outside looking at buildings when it is hot; when you go inside, in some cases it is a riot of forms. The exteriors are severe, but the interiors of Moroccan or Egyptian houses, for example, are beautiful. Filigrees and cut-metal lighting fixtures create a remarkable variety of patterns and lighting.

PRECEDING PAGES The view from a space near the galleries, looking down into the atrium. Discrete stainless steel handrails and a glass barrier facilitate the view downwards.

RIGHT The view down toward the double stairway of the atrium and the decorative patterns on the floor, inspired by geometric Islamic designs.

> "THE DECORATIVE ART OF ISLAM – THE COMPLEXITY OF THE GEOMETRY – IS ABSOLUTELY SUPERB AND I DID NOT KNOW THAT. I WOULD HAVE CREATED MORE DECORATIVE PATTERNS IF I HAD HAD MORE COURAGE." **I. M. PEI**

The big chandelier was inspired in Doha by that." Pei admits that his penchant for decorative forms has gone somewhat further within the Museum than in much of his earlier work, but, he says: "The exterior is also complex in Doha." One of the final touches I. M. Pei made to the interior decor was for the top-floor dining room, which he had left essentially unadorned until a restaurateur was selected. He has designed a series of sixteen faceted stainless-steel ring fixtures that will hang from the ceiling. Although these are more like hanging sculptures than lamps, Pei explains that he was inspired in this instance by "Byzantium, where the lamps are very low so that the priests can light them. The space is huge but the lighting makes it seem intimate." In a museum intended for the decorative arts, his concluding remark on the interiors he designed is particularly pertinent: "The decorative art of Islam – the complexity of the geometry – is absolutely superb and I did not know that. I would have created more decorative patterns if I had had more courage."

## What Is the Best that You Can Find?

Pei's references to the architecture of Islam will undoubtedly find a resonance with visitors from the region, but, as has been the case in his earlier work, the architect has made his design accessible, in every sense of the term, to those who know about history and to those who do not. By including a large Education Centre in the complex, the client signalled the desire to attract all ages to the Museum, children included. Visitors to the Museum, whether foreign or local, will find generous volumes and an awe-inspiring sense of space and materials that few architects could have orchestrated in these ways. The point here is that Pei's architecture will easily attract both the general public and a more deeply cultured audience. The universal or 'human' quali-

ties of the art itself, often originally intended for day-to-day use, find their logical counterpart in the architecture, which is in itself rare enough in the contemporary world to merit being pointed out.

Pei is, of course, faithful to his sense of geometry and to the wealth of possibilities that it offers, especially in forms such as circles, squares and octagons, rotated and exploited to create varied perspectives and unexpected patterns. "From the circle to the square and from the square to the octagon," he repeats, in describing the design of the fountain of Ibn Tulun, but also his own architecture in Doha. Seeking the essence of Islamic architecture and correctly finding it in a ninth-century Cairo mosque or its thirteenth-century

ABOVE Looking down from the upper level to the ground-level café beneath Pei's 45-metre window. The furniture visible here was designed for the Museum by Jean-Michel Wilmotte.

fountain, Pei reveals, as he has in so many other cases, particularly from the Louvre onwards, a deep and significant attachment to the past. More importantly, he has attempted to re-weave the links between the past and the present that have informed architecture throughout history. The geometry, or simplicity, of Modernism was seen from the first as a clean break with the ornamental past. Pei delves further into ornament in Doha than in most of his earlier work, but he clearly does not abandon his passion for geometry. In Doha, his point has certainly not been to create an enlarged replica of the fountain of Ibn Tulun. His view of light, as it falls in the great crescent from Morocco to the Arabian Gulf, and his understanding of geometry as the key to form, variety and expression in architecture bridge the gap opened by the early Modernists who sought in many ways to set aside tradition. When asked if he is seeking in a sense to interpret tradition, he says firmly: "You have to be modern as well, you cannot just go back to history. There is the past, but also everything that has happened since. What is the best that you can find?"

1 The Yuan Dynasty, lasting officially from 1271 to 1368, followed the Song Dynasty and preceded the Ming Dynasty.
2 Mi Fu or Mi Fei (1051–07), scholar, poet, calligrapher and painter, was a dominant figure in Chinese art.
3 Interview with I. M. Pei by the author, 4 November 2006, New York.
4 Interview with I. M. Pei by the author, 27 March 2007, Paris.
5 Interview with I. M. Pei by the author, 4 November 2006, New York.
6 Ibid.
7 Interview with I. M. Pei by the author, 27 March 2007, Paris.
8 Interview with I. M. Pei by the author, 4 November 2006, New York.

"THE INTERIOR DESIGN CLEARLY TAKES AS ITS POINT OF DEPARTURE THE ARCHITECTURE, BUT SO, TOO, IT WAS CONCEIVED WITH RESPECT TO THE VARIETY OF ISLAMIC ART TO BE DISPLAYED, RANGING IN SCALE FROM JEWELS TO LARGE CARPETS." **I. M. PEI**

## Completing a Work of Art

The noted French architect and interior designer Jean-Michel Wilmotte was given the task of creating the exhibition displays for the Museum, but he went on to design all of the furniture and signage, as well as spaces such as the ground-floor shop. Working closely with the architect I. M. Pei and with the Museum, he has succeeded in creating very sophisticated, minimalist galleries that truly allow the objects to come forward in what he describes as a "theatrical" way.

Born in 1948, a graduate of the École Camondo in Paris (1973), Jean-Michel Wilmotte created his own firm, Governor, in 1975. He came to wider attention when he won a competition, organized in 1987 by the public authority responsible for renovating the Louvre (Établissement public du Grand Louvre), for temporary exhibition spaces, a bookshop and restaurants in the area beneath I. M. Pei's Pyramid in the Cour Napoléon of the Louvre. Jean-Michel Wilmotte has spoken of these spaces and of his close work with I. M. Pei and with the associated French architect Michel Macary in these terms: "The work on the first phase of the Louvre project was undertaken on the basis of an extremely precise and detailed programme. It permitted me to have a very interesting dialogue with Pei and Macary. I wanted to go in the same direction as they did and to keep the spirit of the Louvre in mind. I think it was appropriate in this instance to keep a reserved attitude once I had fully assimilated the existing architecture. This is not to say that I attempted in any way to dilute the personality of my work with respect to that of my colleagues." As the completed spaces in the Louvre showed, Wilmotte succeeded in creating a code of interior design that was at once in harmony with the architecture, and yet also sufficiently strong and precise to speak for itself.

Subsequent to his projects in the Louvre with I. M. Pei in the late 1980s and early 1990s, Jean-Michel Wilmotte became one of the most active and influen-

tial interior designers in the museum field in Europe, but, as of 1993, he also began to work as an architect in his own right, while carrying out numerous urban design projects such as the 1994 refurbishment of the Champs-Elysées in Paris. He is currently working on museums in Korea, China, Lebanon, Luxembourg and Bahrain, as well as the celebrated Rijksmuseum in Amsterdam, where he is responsible for 12,000 square metres of renovated exhibition space.

## At the Request of I. M. Pei

Jean-Michel Wilmotte emphasizes his relationship with the architect of the Museum when asked exactly how he came to be involved in the Doha project. "It was quite simply at the request of I. M. Pei and with the encouragement of Luis Monreal that I became involved. I have known I. M. for quite some time, and I believe that in the context of this complex project he did not wish to call on architects with whom he had not worked in the past. We have an easy, natural rapport and that has greatly facilitated the process." Since the essential forms of the building and its interior volumes were comprehensively laid out by I. M. Pei, the intervention of Wilmotte and his team, headed by Emmanuel Brélot, consisted in creating a fundamental unity between the outside of the building, the main public spaces, such as the entrance hall designed by Pei, and the galleries or other areas that were essentially empty shells. "The architecture and the programme have remained unchanged since I. M. Pei

LEFT A display case in the middle of a gallery rises to the ceiling, although the objects displayed within may not be of substantial size. The non-reflective glass employed almost disappears entirely under certain angles.

> "THE CENTRAL SPACE OF EACH GALLERY IS GENERALLY RESERVED FOR LARGE GLASS SHOWCASES OR OBJECTS ON OPEN DISPLAY." **I. M. PEI**

conceived the Museum's plan," explains Wilmotte. "We worked on a total of eighteen rooms laid out in a geometric pattern around a patio on two and a half levels of the structure. Insofar as the exhibition galleries are concerned, there is a total of 5000 square metres of floor area plus another 700 square metres for temporary shows. We also designed the bookshop and the administrative offices of the Museum. I created a full line of minimalist furniture and light fixtures for the entire Museum and we also developed the signage and visual identity for the institution."

The interior design clearly takes the architecture as its point of departure, but so, too, it was conceived with respect to the variety of Islamic art to be displayed, ranging in scale from jewels to large carpets. In contrast with the very recent nature of the building and the display installations, the objects are, of course, very ancient in most cases, sometimes requiring extremely subtle lighting to bring out their originally intense hues and patterns. The architecture of the galleries responds to this challenge with a combination of minimalist design and rare materials. The dark architectural finishes are intended not to intrude on the delicate intricacy of the objects. The galleries have a number of large showcases recessed into the walls, but each one is individualized through variations in the showcase design and different textures applied to the finishes of the cladding materials. The central space of each gallery is generally reserved for large glass showcases or objects on open display. Using unusually large panes of non-reflective glass, the gallery design revolves around the idea of making the display cases so large that they almost disappear, becoming a "form of architecture in and of themselves," as their designer puts it. "We are using an anti-reflection glass in panes that are up to four and a half metres high and three metres wide for the first time in a museum," he says. As Wilmotte explains with undisguised

pride, sometimes the glass becomes invisible, rising from the floor to the ceiling, allowing an unimpeded view of the objects, which almost appear to float in space.

## A Theatrical Atmosphere

I. M. Pei's scheme called for natural light to be essentially reserved for the dramatic entrance volume. As Jean-Michel Wilmotte explains: "The exhibition rooms have no natural light and I decided to create what I would call a theatrical atmosphere in the best sense of the term – an atmosphere that truly allows the objects to be seen and appreciated. I. M. Pei has used a light coloured limestone for the floors of his areas, much as he did in the Louvre, and in the Miho Museum in Japan. I chose dark grey porphyry for all of the

ABOVE Highly sophisticated fibre-optic lighting allows each object to be fully lit, without any of the inconvenience associated with more traditional incandescent lighting systems.

exhibition galleries. On the walls, we used an exotic wood called louro faya that has a naturally visible grain or spotted appearance. The wood was metal brushed and treated with a gilt bronze powder that gives it a metallic appearance and makes it darker than it is at the outset." Although Jean-Michel Wilmotte has been working on museum design for a number of years, and for roughly twenty years with Pei, he underlines the ways in which his own thinking has evolved. "The work at the Louvre for primitive art was the starting point of the presentation in Doha, but I think we have brought a number of technical and aesthetic improvements to the new design that I am particularly proud of. We are using a sophisticated electronic system that permits the curators to open the exhibition cases without actually being obliged to touch the large glass doors. We were also able to distance the power sources from the fibre-optic lighting systems in the displays, greatly reducing the heat generated near the objects," he explains. The very high degree of sophistication of the interior design, signalled by the play of stone or metal against wood, or the variety of surface effects employed, places this design almost in a category by itself amongst world museums. And yet the very concept of the gallery spaces is that the precious cladding materials and display cases should disappear entirely to make way for the objects. The interior design serves the objects above all.

RIGHT Display cases, often recessed into the gallery walls, are intended to almost disappear around the object they protect and put forward.

## Flexibility for the Future

The ongoing formation of the Museum's collection has meant that the very basis for the exhibitions has evolved in the course of the interior design work. This challenge as been met through the very design of the galleries and exhibitions. Wilmotte underlines this flexibility in describing the final results: "The presentation of objects in Doha remains much less dense than it is in a museum such as the Louvre for example. At the outset, we were dealing with 250 to 300 works altogether. That number has now risen to about 500, but with 5000 metres of exhibition space we still have a great deal of leeway. Each work will have the space it merits. I have also been able to provide a very flexible system that will allow the exhibitions to be changed considerably in the future without any difficulty. There was some hesitation about whether to adopt a chronologically based presentation or one centred on materials. In either instance, the display facilities are perfectly well adjusted to giving the best possible environment to the art. There are tables with grey porphyry surfaces measuring seven metres by one and a half metres that were conceived to be able to hold display cases of varying number and size."

The Wilmotte team worked not only on the permanent galleries but also on the temporary exhibition spaces, creating one very large room that can be divided using moveable walls. Floor and ceiling grids allow for very adaptable lighting arrangements, augmented here by custom-designed track lights. Despite its minimalist appearance, this 5.5-metre-high space with resin floors is conceived with complete flexibility in mind. The gift shop of the museum blends in a comfortable way with Pei's grand atrium. Indeed, Wilmotte extends Pei's signature French limestone floors beyond the atrium itself and into the entry of the shop. The dark ambiance of the galleries is introduced here with custom-designed furniture and lighting fixtures, perhaps evoking a library as much as a bookshop. Steel mesh is employed, giving a particularly modern feeling to the space. In the whole of the Museum, including the offices and Education Wing, the furniture was custom designed. Specific wood veneers and leathers were developed for the project to blend with the architecture of the building. One range of materials was selected for the smaller offices, and another for the public spaces. Playing on strong contrasts as he often does, Wilmotte designed an executive office on the upper level of the building entirely with white granite, almost the polar opposite of the dark porphyry seen in the exhibition galleries. Throughout the museum, and the Education Centre, state-of-the-art connections have been provided for computers, video screens and every other conceivable electronic device. It is not an understatement to say that this may well be the most sophisticated and complete museum design project ever carried out. And yet this fact may well escape many visitors who will be drawn inevitably and rightly to the objects. Despite his own strong personality and drive, Jean-Michel Wilmotte has placed himself at the service of a project that concerns architecture and art. In this way, his design has become an integral part of a whole, coming very close to realizing the dream of the Bauhaus, where it was hoped to bring together design and craftsmanship, architecture and art.

## A Gesture of Openness

Bringing together the talents of I.M. Pei and Jean-Michel Wilmotte, the Doha Museum of Islamic Art takes its rightful place amongst the most significant cultural buildings of the early twenty-first century. Even more important, it is a symbol of openness and pride in the culture of Islam, born of civilizations and cultures that span almost half the globe. The architects made their journey to Doha so that others can follow in their footsteps, understanding the fundamental links across time and space that unite cultures and peoples, past and present.

# ARCHITECTURAL DECORATION

In the medieval period the Islamic world spanned an enormous area – thousands of kilometres from Spain in the west to India and Central Asia in the east. Contained within it were dramatically different climates and sharply contrasting natural resources. These differences led to a wide range of architectural traditions distinguished not only by the forms of buildings but also by the materials used for construction and the decoration then applied.

Where good quality building stone was plentiful (Egypt, Syria, Turkey, India) or where money was no object, carved stone was favoured. Marble and other fine decorative stones could be transported large distances by sea and navigable rivers to provide the material for finely carved decoration in key places – capitals on top of columns, or slabs to line the walls of palaces.

Where brick architecture was the norm (Iraq, Iran, Central Asia), fine decoration depended on the skilful working of more humble materials – carved or moulded plaster, for example, or painted tiles. Tiles are a natural decoration for brick architecture – a tile being essentially a brick with a decorative layer of glaze and painting.

Wood was the most widely traded architectural material, essential almost everywhere either for the structure of buildings themselves, or as scaffolding used during construction. Fine woods, however, lent themselves to detailed carving, and were used for doors, shutters and furniture.

**PANEL**

ORIGIN
Iraq (possibly Samarra)

DATE
9th century

MATERIAL
Stucco

DIMENSIONS
84 x 84 cm

NUMBER
SW.15.1999

01 The labour-saving properties of moulded stucco were ideally suited to the rapid growth of the city of Samarra in the ninth century. Large-scale building took place in an astonishingly short period of time, and architectural decoration moved from being carved to moulded. The abstraction and even patterning of the Samarra style made it suitable for any number of architectural contexts and it is possible to see the beginnings of the ubiquitous arabesque emerging from these abstracted vegetal forms.

**CAPITAL**

ORIGIN
Spain, Cordoba (probably Madinat al-Zahra)

DATE
c. 975

MATERIAL
Carved marble

DIMENSIONS
H 30; W 40 cm

NUMBER
SW.151.2008

02 In the tenth century the city of Cordoba, capital of the Spanish Arab Umayyad dynasty, reached its apogee. The palace-city of Madinat al-Zahra (apparently named after a favourite concubine) was built by the great Caliph Abd al-Rahman III and lay on the outskirts of Cordoba. It was comprised of over 100 hectares of palaces and gardens, pavilions, pools and fountains, mosques and markets. Almost nothing but archaeological remains and architectural fragments, such as this capital, remain now, but these traces still evoke the splendour and luxury of the court.

03 This impressive stucco head of a male figure is a rare example of a three-dimensional human representation in the medieval Islamic world. It is attributable to the Seljuk period, in which such figural representation is known to have been produced, and was probably used in the decoration of a palace. The remains of blue on the richly decorated crown indicate that such statues were once coloured.

**HEAD FROM A STATUE**

ORIGIN
Iran (Rayy?)

DATE
c. 1200

MATERIAL
Stucco, paint

DIMENSIONS
H 22 cm

NUMBER
SW.74.2003

**STAR TILE**

ORIGIN
Iran (Kashan)

DATE
c. 1261

MATERIAL
Fritware, lustre painting

DIMENSIONS
Ø 30.5 cm

NUMBER
TI.36.1998

04 Rulers in Iran during the Ilkhanid dynasty developed a passion for architectural decoration in palaces and tombs, and in the 1260s there was a renewed surge in tile production. They were usually produced in the kilns at Kashan, one of the primary ceramic centres of the period. Lustre painted or monochrome glazed star-and-cross tiles, a style adopted from the earlier Seljuk period, was a popular method for decorating the dado panels of tombs. This star tile comes from a famous group of approximately 160 surviving star-and-cross lustre tiles that were installed in the tomb of Imamzade Yahya at Varamin in the early 1260s.

05 These doors, made for the late Seljuk rulers of Anatolia, show a characteristic form of the palmette and split-leaf arabesque. The general geometrical style of the door, however, belongs to a tradition that dates back to pre-Islamic times and is formed by straight framing pieces which hold decorated polygonal panels. In this case, with a plentiful supply of timber, the door was constructed of solid planks, with the design carved across them.

The inscription in the upper panels reads: "The wise one is he who has learnt a lesson from experience; and the ignorant one is he who does not think of the consequences." This suggests that the doors may have come from a bathhouse or other secular building, rather than from a mosque or tomb, where a Qur'anic quotation might be expected.

**PAIR OF DOORS OR WINDOW SHUTTERS**

ORIGIN
Anatolia (Konya)

DATE
c. 1270

MATERIAL
Walnut wood, carved

DIMENSIONS
165 x 115.5 cm

NUMBER
WW.56. 2003

**OCTAGONAL PANEL**

ORIGIN
Egypt (Cairo)

DATE
c. 1296–99

MATERIAL
Wood, carved

DIMENSIONS
Ø 25.6 cm

NUMBER
WW.38.2000

06 This octagonal panel carved in high relief with a vegetal pattern comes from a Mamluk pulpit (*minbar*). Panels similar in style and size can be found on the *minbar* of Sultan al-Mansur Husam al-Din Lajin (ruled 1296–99) made for the mosque of Ibn Tulun in Cairo. The mosque is famous for the story that relates how, early in his career, Lajin hid in the then abandoned and ruined mosque after an unsuccessful attempt to assassinate the ruler. He vowed that if he survived and came to power he would restore the mosque. On succeeding to the sultanate he fulfilled his promise, refurbishing the early Tulunid building and providing an elaborately carved *minbar*.

**07** These panels come from the Agra or Delhi region of India, and probably once adorned the walls or niches of a shrine. Based on the inscription, which reads "Allah, Muhammad, Abu Bakr, 'Umar, 'Uthman, 'Ali, Hasan, Husain", they are likely to be Shi'ite in orientation. Such inscriptions, executed in overlapping and mirrored monumental Thuluth script, were in demand from Shi'ite patrons both in the north and south into the Deccan. Indian Shi'ites were typically of Iranian origin, and were active patrons of shrines around the Delhi and Agra region, becoming fairly numerous by the seventeenth and eighteenth centuries.

**INSCRIPTION PANELS**

ORIGIN
India

DATE
18th century

MATERIAL
Red sandstone, carved

DIMENSIONS
77 x 92 cm

NUMBER
SW.60

# CARPETS AND TEXTILES

It is difficult for us now to grasp the importance of textiles in the medieval Islamic world. Textiles were by far the most important manufactured commodity – made in vast quantities and traded far and wide. Ibn Battuta, like other medieval travellers, saw on sale in the markets of Egypt and Syria textiles from all over the Middle East, from North Africa, the Yemen and Iran, as well as cottons from India and, most expensive of all, silks from China.

It was textiles that underpinned much of the economy of towns and villages; it was in textiles that a man of whatever class would portray his status and wealth through the clothes he wore, or the furnishings of his house; it was in textiles that he could store up wealth for the future, or for the dowries of his daughters.

Islamic textiles were made in an astonishing range of techniques, some of extraordinary complexity with intricate figural designs. From the earliest period they were sought after in the Christian West as articles of the utmost luxury.

Carpets are made with a particular weaving technique, where 'knots' of wool or silk are woven into the base textile to provide a thick, resilient and decorative pile. In the Middle East these were the essential articles of furniture in palace and modest home alike; in Europe they were too highly valued to be used on the floor, but instead were used as table covers.

## TIRAZ

ORIGIN
Egypt

DATE
Mid 10th century

MATERIAL
Linen, woven in red and mustard yellow silk thread

DIMENSIONS (EACH PANEL)
L 52 cm

NUMBER
TR.45.2003

08 The word *tiraz* originates from the Persian word for 'embroidery' and came to refer to lengths of cloth and garments with inscriptions. The Abbasid government, which held a monopoly over *tiraz* manufacturing, used them mainly for prestigious robes or as gifts. A *tiraz* band of either embroidered or woven inscription was usually placed on the upper sleeves of a robe or on a turban sash and showed that the wearer was either a prince, or had been granted an honour by one. It is likely that this *tiraz*, typically decorated with bold Kufic, was made during the reign of al-Muti (ruled 946–974). The inscription reads: "Bism'illah al-rahman al-rahim al-M[uti li'llah ...]".

**09** This set of six textile panels was commissioned as the furnishing for the interior of a majestic tent. Under Mongol rule in Iran, mobile courts were favoured in order to move easily to congenial locations, adapting to the seasons. Rulers set up large encampments, which were lavishly decorated in textiles. These panels demonstrate the quality of weaving achieved under Mongol patronage, the enormous expense of large quantities of gold thread, and the intriguing combination of styles derived from the different artistic traditions of Iran and China.

**TENT PANELS**

ORIGIN
Central Asia

DATE
13th century

MATERIAL
Silk lampas,
woven in gold and red

DIMENSIONS
(EACH PANEL)
H 234 cm; Ø 123 cm

NUMBER
TE.40.2002

**ROBE**

ORIGIN
Central Asia

DATE
13th century

MATERIAL
Silk, woven with gold thread

DIMENSIONS
Neck to hem: 130 cm; end of sleeve to midline: 98 cm

NUMBER
CO.111.2000

10 Nomads of Central Asia treasured textiles and used them to convey status. These portable luxuries were often woven in gold thread as a means of transporting their wealth. The Mongols continued this tradition, often covering almost the entire textile in gold. Gold thread was made by beating the gold very thin and wrapping it in a spiral around a 'core' silk thread. The silk core made the thread much lighter, more flexible and less breakable. Garments made of cloth-of-gold were worn by those in the highest ranks of Mongol society. The cut of this robe is typically Mongol with its full skirt (worn with trousers) for riding, its broad left-over-right wrap-over, and the extremely long sleeves.

11 This very rare and unusually shaped carpet (as near to round as the weavers were able to make it) was probably made for the European market as a table cover. Carpets imported from the Middle East in this early period were considered to be far too rare and precious to place on the floor (where they would be walked on) and were used as hangings or table covers. Despite its atypical shape, this carpet is in archetypal Mamluk style characterized by intricate centralized designs, executed in red, green, blue and yellow and with the presence of one or more large octagonal medallions. The entire field is densely decorated with geometrical motifs composed of octagons, hexagons, triangles and stars which create a stunning, kaleidoscopie visual effect that some believe has similarities with Tibetan Buddhist mandalas.

**ROUND CARPET**

ORIGIN
Egypt (Cairo)

DATE
c. 1575

MATERIAL
Wool

DIMENSIONS
282 x 270 cm

NUMBER
TE.7.1997

**HANGING WITH INSCRIPTIONS**

ORIGIN
Spain

DATE
15th century

MATERIAL
Silk lampas, woven

DIMENSIONS
386 x 270 cm

NUMBER
TE.6.1999

12 The design of this hanging resembles closely the decoration of the Alhambra palace in Granada and other Nasrid buildings. It looks like an ornate wooden door with fabric 'panels' of Naskhi calligraphic script. An example of this can be seen beneath the row of arches at the top in white on a red ground which reads "There is no victor except God", the Nasrid motto. Conducting official business and receiving guests in curtained and draped surroundings secluded the caliph from his subjects and was an indication of great prestige and status.

**CUSHION COVER**

ORIGIN
Turkey (Bursa)

DATE
17th century

MATERIAL
Cut voided silk velvet with precious metal thread

DIMENSIONS
116 x 66 cm

NUMBER
TE.11.1997

13 Ottoman textiles display a great variety of designs and cover the whole aesthetic range typical of Ottoman art, from the highly ornate to the austere. This bold and simple pattern relies for its effect on the repetition of the single strong carnation motif offset in gold thread against a rich red velvet ground. Cushions were an important part of the furnishings of domestic interiors, where there was no mobile furniture.

14 The 'spots and stripes' motif was particularly popular during the Ottoman period. The stripes are associated with power: it is believed that the origins of the design came from a time when kings and high-ranking men used to wear the skins of powerful animals, such as tigers and leopards. The triple-circle motif had associations beyond that of power and kingship for it had long been used to represent the Buddhist, eternal, wish-granting jewel or *çintamani*. In Ottoman times the two devices were often used together to form a powerful repeating pattern.

## ÇINTAMANI VELVET

ORIGIN
Turkey (Bursa)

DATE
c. 1550

MATERIAL
Silk velvet,
silver-wrapped silk thread

DIMENSIONS
83 x 63 cm

NUMBER
TE.29.1998

**THE 'FRANCHETTI' TAPESTRY**

ORIGIN
Iran (Kashan)

DATE
c. 1575

MATERIAL
Silk and silver-wrapped silk thread on a silver foundation

DIMENSIONS
219 x 151 cm

NUMBER
CA.2.1997

15 In the early Safavid period, designs involving animals and mythical beasts are found in all decorative arts. This 'animal style' was developed in the eastern Iranian lands in the fifteenth century. The animals depicted in this tapestry have a variety of origins. Some, such as the phoenix and the *qilin* (a deer-like creature of good omen), derive ultimately from China. In addition to these exotic creatures we find others drawn from an ancient indigenous tradition, such as the bird of paradise which resembles a peacock.

16 The arts in Iran flourished under the patronage of Shah Tahmasp (ruled 1524–76). This high-quality silk carpet was probably made for courtly use during his reign. The carpet has a completely abstract decor with a central, cloud-fringed 'medallion' floating on a ground of scattered flowers linked together by delicate tracery. We do not know if abstract designs of this type were imbued with meaning by the people who designed them; some recent scholars speculate that the design reflects a religious iconography. Its similarity to designs for bookbinding and manuscript illumination suggest that it originated in the royal design studio.

**THE 'ROTHSCHILD' CARPET**

ORIGIN
Iran (Kashan)

DATE
Mid 16th century

MATERIAL
Silk pile on a silk foundation

DIMENSIONS
234 x 177 cm

NUMBER
CA.21.1999

**'LAILA AND MAJNUN' TAPESTRY**

ORIGIN
Iran (possibly Kashan)

DATE
Late 16th–
early 17th century

MATERIAL
Silk tapestry

DIMENSIONS
179 x 129 cm

NUMBER
CA.1.1997

**17** Woven in silk by using the tapestry technique, this is a magnificent and unique example of a large-scale figural work depicting a narrative scene. It illustrates an episode in the popular love story of Laila and Majnun. Taken from Arab folklore, the story was adapted by the twelfth-century Persian poet, Nizami, and is usually illustrated in miniature painting. Here, the lovelorn Majnun (the 'mad one'), having retreated as a hermit to the desert, is brought before his beloved.

## THE 'HYDERABAD' CARPET

ORIGIN
India (Hyderabad)

DATE
17th century

MATERIAL
Wool pile on cotton foundation

DIMENSIONS
1596 x 325 cm

NUMBER
CA.017.1997

18 This exceptionally large carpet is one of the most important carpets of its period to have survived. Significant capital investment was needed to employ highly skilled craftsmen, to buy vast amounts of expensive coloured wool and to set up the loom for a carpet of this scale; this and the quality of weaving all indicate royal patronage. The intricacy of design, attention to detail and absence of pattern repetition suggest the design may have been supplied by royal painters or illuminators.

### VELVET WITH FEMALE FIGURES

ORIGIN
Iran (probably Kashan)

DATE
Mid 17th century

MATERIAL
Silk velvet, wrapped silk, silk embroidery

DIMENSIONS
197 x 57 cm

NUMBER
TE.1.1997

19 The large size of the repeat image, the multiple textures and the remarkable range of colours put this piece amongst the great achievements of Islamic weaving; it is also in astonishingly good condition. Such textiles were often cut up to make coats in Safavid Iran and it is recorded that these figurative coats shocked the more Orthodox Ottomans. This example has been altered in some places in order to change the role of the female figures: later embroidery has changed the wine flasks and cups they carry into flower vases.

# PAINTINGS AND CALLIGRAPHY

Painting in the Islamic world means almost exclusively illustrations in manuscripts. The important tradition of wall decoration hardly survives at all in buildings: ironically the little we know about it comes mostly from illustrations in manuscripts.

Islamic painting was not an independent art, as in China or Europe. Instead, it was one of the several arts needed to make a fine book: paper-making, illuminating, binding and calligraphy. Calligraphy was always the most important art, and calligraphers were artist-celebrities long before the identity of painters became important.

Calligraphers did not just produce books, but also government documents and inscriptions for buildings and works of art. Calligraphy was the first Islamic art, as copies of the Qur'an in sumptuous form were produced from the earliest times. Parchment (prepared skin of calves, sheep and goats) was gradually replaced by cheaper paper, introduced from China, from the eighth century.

Book illustration is a very particular form of painting, constrained not just by the page size, but also by the close relationship to the text. The paintings are not considered alone, but are found as the reader turns the page where they highlight key moments in the text.

Independent paintings are a late development, made specifically for albums of calligraphy, painting and illumination. Large-scale oil painting only developed in response to seeing European work, and did not become important until the nineteenth century.

Illuminators, a distinct craft, were skilled in gilding and painting the non-representational decoration of books, and probably for the design of similar patterns found elsewhere.

**PAGES FROM A QUR'AN IN HIJAZI SCRIPT**

ORIGIN
Arabian Peninsula or Syria

DATE
7th–early 8th century

MATERIAL
Ink on parchment

DIMENSIONS (EACH PAGE)
33.7 x 25 cm

NUMBER
MS.67.2007

**20** This page represents one of the rarest and earliest written versions of the Qur'an to survive, produced perhaps within decades of the death of the Prophet Muhammad himself. The Hijazi script developed in the Hijaz region of the Arabian Peninsula, which includes the cities of Mecca and Medina. This type of script was already in use at the time of the emergence of Islam, and was used to produce the first written copies of the Qur'an – previously the Holy text had been preserved by memory alone, among the Companions of the Prophet and their followers. One of the earliest scripts, Hijazi does not contain any dots or diacritical marks to distinguish similar letters or vowels. Later, a more strict, formal style was developed from the Hijazi script which became known under the general name of Kufic.

21 This leaf comes from a manuscript that has come to be known as the 'Blue' Qur'an. Written in gold on a dark-blue background, the original manuscript, consisting of some 900 leaves, must have been one of the most sumptuous ever produced. Some scholars speculate that this Qur'an was made as a gift for the Byzantine emperor as there was a tradition amongst the Byzantines for producing high-quality coloured manuscripts. A sumptuous manuscript of Islam's Holy text from the Byzantines' rivals in North Africa would be sure to impress. However, the manuscript appears to have stayed in North Africa, where the largest section of the manuscript is still preserved.

**PAGE FROM A QUR'AN**
SURA AL-BAQARA, 2, VV. 34-41

ORIGIN
North Africa

DATE
10th century

MATERIAL
Gold ink on blue parchment

DIMENSIONS
28 x 38 cm

NUMBER
MS.8.2006

**PAGE FROM THE 'BAYSUNGHUR' QUR'AN**
SURA AL-ANKABUT, 29, VV. 25–27
CALLIGRAPHY ATTRIBUTED TO UMAR-I AQTA

ORIGIN
Central Asia (probably Samarqand or Herat)

DATE
c. 1400–30

MATERIAL
Ink and gold on paper

DIMENSIONS
177 x 101 cm

NUMBER
MS.119.2007

22 This page comes from a unique gigantic Qur'an manuscript from the Timurid period. It was produced either under the patronage of Baysunghur – a grandson of Timur (ruled 1370–1405) – or for Timur himself. Supposedly, the calligrapher Umar-i Aqta had tried to impress Timur by writing a Qur'an so small that it could fit within a signet ring. However, the sultan was not impressed; the calligrapher, disappointed, went away and wrote another copy, this time extremely large. The sultan, this time much impressed, rewarded the calligrapher with great honours. It is indeed an astonishing calligraphic tour de force to maintain a superb script on such a large scale over the long period it would have taken to produce. The finished manuscript consisted of some 1600 unbound sheets: a massive marble Qur'an stand in the courtyard of the Masjid-i Jami in Timur's capital, Samarqand, may have been made to hold it.

**23** The *Shahnama* (Book of Kings) is a poetic opus written by the Persian poet Firdawsi around 1010 that came to be regarded as the national epic of Iran. Illustrated copies of the manuscript date back to the early fourteenth century. Shah Tahmasp's studio in the first half of the sixteenth century gathered together the most highly gifted artists and craftsmen, and books reached new heights of perfection and sophistication. Shah Tahmasp's *Shahnama* is the most splendid of all, and is one of the highest achievements in the art of the book from any land or period. It was the result of more than twenty years work of illumination, painting and calligraphy. In his later years, Shah Tahmasp lost interest in the arts, and this splendid volume was sent as a gift to his great rival, the Ottoman sultan.

**'FERIDOUN CROSSING THE RIVER TIGRIS'**
ILLUSTRATED FOLIO FROM THE *SHAHNAMA* OF SHAH TAHMASP ATTRIBUTED TO SULTAN MUHAMMAD

ORIGIN
Iran (Tabriz)

DATE
c. 1525–35

MATERIAL
Opaque watercolour, ink and gold on paper

DIMENSIONS
27.1 x 20.7 cm

NUMBER
MS.40.2007

**'THE NIGHTMARE OF ZAHHAK'**
ILLUSTRATED FOLIO FROM THE *SHAHNAMA* OF SHAH TAHMASP ATTRIBUTED TO MIR MUSAVVIR

ORIGIN
Iran (Tabriz)

DATE
c. 1525–35

MATERIAL
Opaque watercolour, ink and gold on paper

DIMENSIONS
47 x 32 cm

NUMBER
MS.41.2007

24 This illustration is also from the famous *Shahnama* of Shah Tahmasp. The particular scene shows an episode in the life of the evil king Zahhak. After making a deal with the devil to usurp the throne from his father, Zahhak was cursed with two serpents that grew from his shoulders and fed on human brains. In the scene, a distressed Zahhak is depicted having woken from a nightmare foretelling his own downfall. The confused and distressing perspective of the architecture reflects his frightened state of mind.

25 This is an important work by the royal Safavid artist Mirza 'Ali, who was one of the leading artists of the monumental *Shahnama* produced by the court atelier under Shah Tahmasp. This example and others like it were produced in order to satisfy a fashion for albums, which gathered together examples of fine calligraphy and painting. These were perhaps for patrons who could not afford to commission a complete manuscript and probably provided a livelihood for artists when Shah Tahmasp's interest and patronage of painting had dramatically declined.

**A SEATED YOUTH**
ATTRIBUTED TO MIRZA 'ALI

ORIGIN
Iran (probably Mashhad)

DATE
c. 1570–75

MATERIAL
Opaque watercolour with gold on paper

DIMENSIONS
11.6 x 6.4 cm

NUMBER
MS.32.2007

**'ST JEROME REPRESENTING MELANCHOLY'**
ILLUSTRATION FROM A MUGHAL ROYAL ALBUM SIGNED BY FARRUKH BEG

ORIGIN
India

DATE
Dated AH 1024 [1615]

MATERIAL
Opaque watercolour with ink and gold on paper

DIMENSIONS
39.2 x 25.9 cm

NUMBER
MS.44.2007

26 This painting was made for Emperor Jahangir and mounted in the album of Emperor Shah Jahan. The painting is based on a work by the sixteenth-century European painter Albrecht Dürer, showing an appreciation of the art of other cultures by the Mughal emperors. The fashion for copying European prints or borrowing compositional aspects from them began during the Akbar period, when prints were brought to India by Jesuit missionaries, travellers and emissaries. Farrukh Beg is the ideal painter of such a subject – an unsettled artist who moved to different patrons' ateliers and developed in his style a dark individualism.

27 Western students of Islamic art tend to concentrate on the illustrative paintings; however, other equally sophisticated skills are needed to produce a fine book. The *mudhahhib,* or gilder, was responsible for all the decorative illumination and this page shows what extraordinary skill was required. Islamic manuscripts and albums from Persia and India often opened with a page of radiating illuminated decoration known as a *shamsa* (from the Arabic *shams* – meaning 'sun') designed to create a great visual impact from the very beginning. The exceptional quality of the illumination and the size of this page point to a royal commission, and it has been suggested that this page was made for one of the royal albums of Shah Jahan in the 1640s and 1650s.

**ILLUMINATED SHAMSA**

ORIGIN
India

DATE
c. 1640–50

MATERIAL
Opaque watercolour, ink and gold on paper

DIMENSIONS
38 x 27.4 cm

NUMBER
MS.53.2007

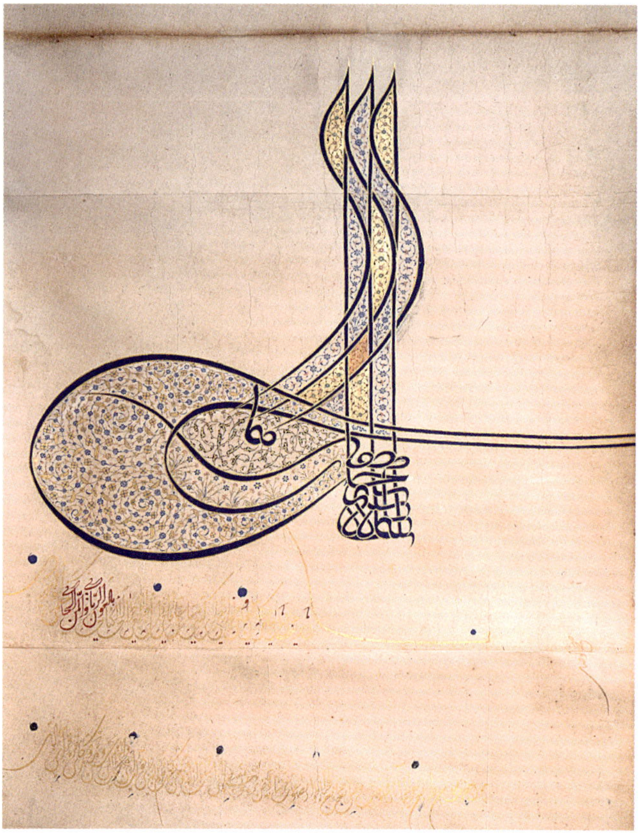

**DECREE OF SULTAN SULEYMAN THE MAGNIFICENT**

ORIGIN
Turkey (Istanbul)

DATE
Dated AH 966 [1559–60]

MATERIAL
Ink, pigments and gold on paper

DIMENSIONS
295 x 59.5 cm

NUMBER
MS.1.1997

28 This royal decree is a masterpiece of Ottoman calligraphy. It declares the conferment of a palace in Istanbul by Sultan Suleyman the Magnificent (ruled 1520–66) on his granddaughter. It is headed by the sultan's *tughra* – his name and titles in calligraphic form. The *tughra* served as the insignia of the sultan, identifying him on documents, monuments, coins and elsewhere. It was designed at the beginning of each Ottoman sultan's reign by the court calligrapher, and the basic form remained throughout his reign, though the size and ornamentation depended on the context.

This decree is particularly distinct in terms of its scale and lavishness: the blue script outlined in gold and the spiralling illumination mark it as an imperial degree of the highest importance.

29 By the seventeenth century, the previously unfamiliar technique of painting in oil on canvas was beginning to become popular at court, due to extended contacts with the West. The style of painting, however, remained indigenous, with the paintings struggling to break away from the more two-dimensional rendering typical of Islamic book illustration. Hierarchical postures and poses created a new figural ideal, which also flattered the facial characteristics of the Qajars. The long black beards are typical for this period.

**PORTRAIT OF HASAN ALI MIRZA SHUJA AL-SALTANA**

ORIGIN
Iran (Tehran)

DATE
c. 1810–15

MATERIAL
Oil on canvas

DIMENSIONS
176.5 x 99 cm

NUMBER
PA.4.2004

# CERAMICS

The development of a widespread glazed-pottery industry producing decorative and luxury items on a large scale is a striking feature of the Islamic period.

Previously in the Middle East, domestic pottery had consisted entirely of unsophisticated unglazed vessels. However, by as early as the beginning of the ninth century AD, glazed pottery in myriad forms was made at countless centres across the Islamic world, from Spain to Central Asia. This is an astonishing historical event: only in China was ceramic production, developed over many centuries, more advanced.

An explosion of invention and productivity started in the central Islamic lands – particularly Egypt and Iraq – and spread rapidly to the very borders. The skills and 'know-how' were probably taken by potters who migrated with their families to set up workshops in new places. Customers for the new wares were found everywhere, but the driving force was the enormous populations that grew up in both ancient and newly founded cities and that are a striking feature of the early Islamic period.

Islamic potters used simple materials and techniques and did not have access to the high-firing porcelain clays of China, whose luxury imports were much admired and copied.

However, Islamic potters exploited, earlier and to a greater extent than any other potters, the particular qualities of low-fired earthenware: seemingly limitless colours and a multitude of decorative techniques enabling the production of unlimited patterns.

## BOWL

ORIGIN
Iraq (probably Basra)

DATE
9th century

MATERIAL
Earthenware, white glaze with painting in blue

DIMENSIONS
Ø 20.5 cm

NUMBER
PO.31.1999

30 From the late eighth century, Chinese porcelains were imported into the Middle East where they were traded as highly luxurious goods. Potters in Iraq soon began to develop imitations of these highly prized porcelains, using earthenware with an opaque white glaze. The decoration on the bowl, however, is a local innovation; painted in blue, an inscription is written radially and asymmetrically and reads "made by Salih", or alternatively "what was done was worthwhile". The restrained, somewhat austere decoration provides a counterpoint to the highly decorated aesthetic often seen to typify Islamic art.

31 Epigraphic wares are examples of an aesthetic interest in calligraphy for both its decorative and expressive qualities. Samanid examples are typically decorated in black on a white slip ground, perhaps copying silver dishes with similar decoration of black niello on the polished silver. The inscriptions illustrate the social and literary interests of the dishes' owners. Usually consisting of aphorisms in Arabic and sayings attributed to the Prophet and his successors, the text here is a proverb attributed to Yahya ibn Ziyad: "Foolish is the person who misses his chance and afterwards reproaches fate". The inscription is revealed as the contents are eaten – providing an exemplary 'conversation piece' with which to conclude a social gathering of scholars.

**DISH**

ORIGIN
Iran or Central Asia (Nishapur or Samarqand)

DATE
10th century

MATERIAL
Earthenware, with decoration in black on white slip

DIMENSIONS
Ø 42.5 cm

NUMBER
PO.24.1999

## JUG FILTERS

ORIGIN
Egypt

DATE
11th century

MATERIAL
Earthenware, incised

DIMENSIONS
Maximum Ø 9 cm

NUMBER
PO.226.2004

32 Evidence of the medieval potter's skill and creativity is shown in these examples of everyday earthenware. A disk of clay was carefully pieced with elaborate and complex designs, resembling lacework. The filters were placed inside the jugs during manufacture, at the junction of neck and body, to prevent flies from entering. The jars were not glazed in order to allow the water to seep through the clay walls and evaporate, thus cooling the contents. They were made in their thousands, but of thin delicate clay which broke easily. The filters survive, but the jars themselves usually only survive in small fragments.

33 Lustre is an overglaze painting technique, whereby a mixture of silver and copper oxides fixed in a second firing leaves a decoration of metallic or pearly sheen. The technique first appeared on ceramics in Iraq in the early Abbasid period. Lustre-painted pottery later emerged in Egypt under Fatimid rule, where it was probably introduced through migrating craftsmen from Iraq. This bowl depicts a harpy, a popular motif with the Fatimids. The dotted background is characteristic of earlier lustre designs.

**BOWL**

ORIGIN
Egypt

DATE
12th century

MATERIAL
Earthenware,
with lustre painting

DIMENSIONS
Ø 20.5 cm

NUMBER
PO.200.2003

## DISH

ORIGIN
Signed by Muhammad ibn Abi Tahir
Iran (Kashan)

DATE
Dated AH Shawwal 611 [February 1214]

MATERIAL
Fritware, with lustre painting

DIMENSIONS
Ø 20.5 cm

NUMBER
PO.285.2004

**34** Lustre-painted ceramics have a long history in the Islamic world, with the earliest examples dating to the eighth and ninth centuries. However, it was in late twelfth- and early thirteenth-century Iran that lustre ceramics were brought to an entirely new level of production. Kashan was the principal production site, where potters developed a distinct style of decoration. This exceptional example of a Kashan dish is decorated with a veiled woman riding an elephant. Moreover, it bears a signature which is possibly that of Muhammad ibn Abi Tahir, a famous Kashan potter of the pre-Mongol era, and head of a family who produced lustreware over three generations. The shape of the dish, standing on three feet, is taken from a metalwork shape believed to be used as an incense burner.

35 Figurative decoration on Iranian pottery of the twelfth and thirteenth centuries reflects a contemporary tradition of mural and manuscript painting, of which virtually nothing survives. The repertoire of *mina'i* enamelware sometimes includes recognizable episodes from the epic *Shahnama* and it is possible that the scene depicted on this bowl shows just such a one: the ruler Bahram Chubina is presented with the head of a general, Ayin Ghashap, who was sent to oppose him. The head is being held by the soldier who had murdered the general. However, the soldier has misjudged the ruler; Bahram had great respect for Ayin Ghashap and had the soldier hanged.

**BOWL**

ORIGIN
Iran

DATE
Late 12th–
early 13th century

MATERIAL
Fritware, with enamel painting

DIMENSIONS
H 9.5 cm; Ø 21.6 cm

NUMBER
PO.228.2002

## JAR

ORIGIN
Syria (probably Damascus)

DATE
Late 13th or 14th century

MATERIAL
Fritware, with decoration in blue, black and red glaze

DIMENSIONS
H 36.5 cm

NUMBER
PO.40.1999

36 This jar is one of the most interesting ceramics from Syria to survive. On the shoulder is the word "naufar" (water lily); an inscription around the shoulder states that the piece was made for the "hospital of Nuri", in reference to the famous hospital in Damascus founded in the twelfth century by Nur al-Din Mahmud ibn Zangi. The fleur-de-lis, depicted on the body, was the personal emblem of Nur al-Din, and also of the Mamluk Sultan Qala'un, who was treated and cured at the hospital and then restored it in the late thirteenth century. The jar originally contained a medical preparation made from water lilies, whose qualities are described by traditional pharmacists as being "astringent, demulcent, anodyne, and anti-scrofulous". The pharmacy at the hospital probably contained several dozen such jars and similar albarellos in which to store a wide range of medicine, though this is a unique survivor.

37 The Iznik ceramic industry, which began in the late fifteenth century, was by the mid sixteenth century producing some of the best pottery ever made. Imperial commissions produced the highest quality tiles and vessels, before price restraint and late payment from the court forced the potters to address a more commercial market with wares of lesser quality. This bottle was made at the high point of Iznik's fortunes. Turquoise and blue were popular colour combinations in the mid century, just before the full introduction of bright red and greens.

**BOTTLE**

ORIGIN
Turkey (Iznik)

DATE
C. 1540

MATERIAL
Fritware, with underglaze painting in blue and turquoise

DIMENSIONS
H 37 cm

NUMBER
PO.47.1999

### DISH

ORIGIN
Turkey (Iznik)

DATE
c. 1545–50

MATERIAL
Fritware, underglaze painting in black, blue, turquoise, purple and sage green

DIMENSIONS
H 4.2 cm; Ø 29.6 cm

NUMBER
PO.48.1999

38 The decoration on this dish is typical of Ottoman pottery produced in the town of Iznik in the mid sixteenth century, by which point the rather formal designs of earlier periods had been replaced by more naturalistic floral designs. Flowers such as the carnation, tulip, rose, hyacinth and plum blossom became popular designs and continued to develop later in the century. The colours on this dish represent the most subtle of all Iznik ware; in the mid sixteenth century red was yet to be introduced, and potters were using a more subdued and subtle palette of blue, turquoise, sage and olive greens and purple.

39 A rich palette of blue, black, red and green stands out against an even white ground, and dates the dish to the second half of the sixteenth century when potters introduced the brilliant raised red pigment for which Iznik became famous. The design on the dish pays tribute to the Ottoman passions for flowers and gardens – depicting the ever popular stylized tulips and more lifelike carnations.

**DISH**

ORIGIN
Turkey (Iznik)

DATE
c. 1570–75

MATERIAL
Fritware, with underglaze painting

DIMENSIONS
Ø 26.3 cm

NUMBER
PO.49.1999

# METAL

Metal has been an immensely important material throughout the history of human civilization, not only in the manufacture of eminently practical utensils, but also as a pre-eminent artistic vehicle.

A practical object – a fountain head for example – can become an outstanding work of art: a powerfully and sensitively modelled animal spouting water from its mouth, once gilded to look like solid gold, and a key element in an environment which reflected the power and taste of the ruler. A war mask – once the visor of a helmet – fashioned to inspire friends and terrify enemies. A pen box, not just to hold writing implements, but to signal the status and prestige of a royal advisor. A precise scientific instrument as a thing of beauty.

In the Islamic world, metalworking continued pre-Islamic traditions, but developed styles and techniques of its own. Gold and silver decoration inlaid into brass vessels were a particular contribution. At his most refined, the metalworker presented intricate patterns or scenes of court life, which, in their complexity and artistic skill, were quite the equal of any miniature painter.

While many vessels survive from the past, many more have been lost – victims to rust and corrosion, but particularly to recycling as old-fashioned or worn-out vessels were melted down to provide the raw material for new objects. This is particularly true of objects made from precious metals, silver and gold, once the usual privilege of the elite but which we now mostly know through copies made in cheaper materials.

**FOUNTAIN HEAD**

ORIGIN
Spain

DATE
Mid 10th century

MATERIAL
Bronze, engraved

DIMENSIONS
H 48.1 cm

NUMBER
MW.7.1997

40 Gilded to look like solid gold, this fountain head in the form of a hind (female deer) would have stood beside a basin or pool in a palatial setting in Umayyad Spain with water spurting from its mouth. It was cast in one piece, probably by the 'lost wax' process, where a full-size model is made in wax, which is then coated in clay. The wax is 'lost' when the clay is fired, providing a mould for the molten metal. The creature's surface is covered with decoration seeming to resemble a tasselled textile.

41 Made by al-Khujandi, an eminent mathematician, astronomer and constructor of astronomical instruments, this planispheric astrolabe combines beauty with advanced scientific computations. This is a particularly important piece as it is one of the earliest astrolabes to have survived. The tracery of the star map has pointers for thirty-three stars, including six birds engraved with the names of the stars and the tips of the beaks pointing to their position; it also incorporates a quatrefoil motif found on the star maps of early European astrolabes.

**ASTROLABE**
MADE BY HAMID IBN AL-KHIDR AL-KHUJANDI

ORIGIN
Iran (Rayy) or Iraq (Baghdad)

DATE
Dated AH 374 [984–985]

MATERIAL
Brass, engraved

DIMENSIONS
Ø 15 cm

NUMBER
SI.5.1999

**ASTROLABE**
MADE BY AHMED IBN HUSAIN IBN BASO

ORIGIN
Spain (Granada)

DATE
Dated AH 709 [1309–10]

MATERIAL
Brass

DIMENSIONS
Ø 13.5 cm

NUMBER
MW.342.2007

42 This is one of only three surviving astrolabes made by Ahmed ibn Husain ibn Baso, a well-known astronomer and *muwaqit* (official timekeeper) for the great mosque of Granada. This astrolabe has five plates calibrated for use in Mecca, Oman, Aswan, Alexandria, Granada, Malaga and Algeciras and is inscribed in both Arabic and Latin. The use of Latin demonstrates the movement of Islamic knowledge from East to West with Spain acting as a bridge.

43 Pen boxes, in addition to being practical containers for pens and ink, were of symbolic significance in both court and administrative contexts. This was particularly so under the Mamluk dynasty in Egypt (1250–1517), where the emblem of the pen box represented the Dawadar, an executive secretary or royal messenger who supervised the execution of the sultan's orders. On this prestigious piece, as well as geometric designs and floral scrolls there are depictions of musicians, a lion hunter and an enthroned ruler set in roundels.

## PEN BOX

ORIGIN
Syria or Iraq

DATE
Late 13th century

MATERIAL
Brass, with gold and silver inlay

DIMENSIONS
H 3.9 cm; L 23 cm; W 4.7 cm

NUMBER
MW.121.1999

**KASHKUL**

ORIGIN
Western Iran

DATE
*c.* 1550

MATERIAL
Brass, engraved

DIMENSIONS
H 7.4 cm; L 38 cm

NUMBER
MW.19.1997

44 This form of vessel is derived from a boat-shaped drinking cup, used in pre-Islamic and early Islamic times for wine. It gradually took on Sufi mystic symbolism and, according to the fifteenth-century Persian poet Jami, the crescent shape of the vessel symbolized the moon and the wine poured into it the sun. Although wine is often thought of as an alcoholic drink prohibited by strict Muslims, it also symbolizes the means of achieving 'divine intoxication' in mystic literature.

45 The inscription around the body of this silver and gold inlaid candlestick reveals that it was made for Abu Ishaq Inju, ruler of the Iranian province of Fars (1341–56), whose capital, Shiraz, was a vibrant centre for the arts and where the candlestick is likely to have been made. The artisans of Shiraz were renowned for their workmanship and the chasing and inlay techniques here are of extremely high quality. The body is covered with detailed decoration with substantial figurative representation, including images of Abu Ishaq with his courtiers and his wife with her attendants. There is also a plethora of animals and supernatural creatures.

**CANDLESTICK**

ORIGIN
Iran (Shiraz)

DATE
1341–56

MATERIAL
Brass, engraved and inlaid with gold and silver

DIMENSIONS
H 34.5 cm; Ø 38.2 cm

NUMBER
MW.122.1999

## WAR MASK

ORIGIN
Eastern Turkey or Western Iran

DATE
15th century

MATERIAL
Steel, with gold inlay

DIMENSIONS
H 21 cm; W 18.6 cm

NUMBER
MW.6.1997

46 This gilded mask was originally attached to a helmet. There are also attachments to the chin and eyebrows which were used to connect it to a protective steel 'beard'. The inscription around the face of the mask mentions "al-adan", meaning Eden, a possible allusion to Paradise. Menacing horsemen wearing steel war masks can be seen in late fourteenth-century *Shahnama* illustrations, indicating their widespread use in battle in Iran.

47 This *yataghan*, or 'Turkish sword', commissioned by Sultan Bayezid II for a court official, is probably the earliest datable example of its kind. The shape of the hilt is pre-Islamic indicating a historic manufacturing tradition, whereas the decorative adornment is typical of the austere aesthetic of the Ottoman period, which contrasts with that of the more colourful Iznik pottery.

**SWORD (YATAGHAN) AND SCABBARD**
MADE BY MUSTAFA IBN KEMAL AL-AKSHERI

ORIGIN
Turkey

DATE
1481–1512

MATERIAL
Steel with gold inlay, wood, leather

DIMENSIONS
L 76 cm

NUMBER
AA.6.1997

# JEWELLERY

People have valued gold and silver, and prized rare and colourful stones from prehistoric times.

Such things are used to signal status and wealth in the form of personal adornment in jewellery or as the accoutrements of gracious living, in gold and silver drinking vessels or serving dishes. For the very wealthy, even furniture or architectural ornament can be made of, or be elaborately decorated with, precious metals.

Equally important, these materials can be used to store wealth in a compact and easily portable form – useful for concealment from thieves or tax officials, or, if need be, to aid rapid departure from one place to another when the situation demanded.

Gold and silver can additionally be reworked with little problem from one form to another depending on need: jewellery stripped of its gems, gold vessels remade as coinage. The ease of working gold and silver means that owners need not tolerate old-fashioned styles, but have their vessels and jewellery refashioned into more up-to-date styles.

However, this advantage for the owner is a disadvantage for us now in our interest in the past. From the large quantities of jewellery and precious-metal vessels described in literature, almost nothing survives. What were the commonest things – dishes and vessels, small items of jewellery – are now the rarest. Gems and precious stones survive more frequently, due to the difficulty of reworking them.

**PAIR OF BRACELETS**

ORIGIN
Egypt

DATE
11th–12th century

MATERIAL
Gold, decorated with gold wire, granulation and repoussé

DIMENSIONS
Ø 8 cm

NUMBER
JE.118.2003

48 Both technically and aesthetically, goldwork reached its zenith during the Fatimid dynasty. Jewellery achieved brilliance in its decorative elements, drawing on inspiration from earlier periods. Comparisons can be also made with contemporary enamelled gold jewellery from the Fatimids' great rivals, the Byzantine empire. The custom of adorning the wrists with identical bracelets can be seen in the representations on Fatimid pottery. This pair of bracelets is one of the best known examples of a recognizable type made under Fatimid patronage in Egypt and Syria between the tenth and twelfth century. Similar bracelets were also made in silver.

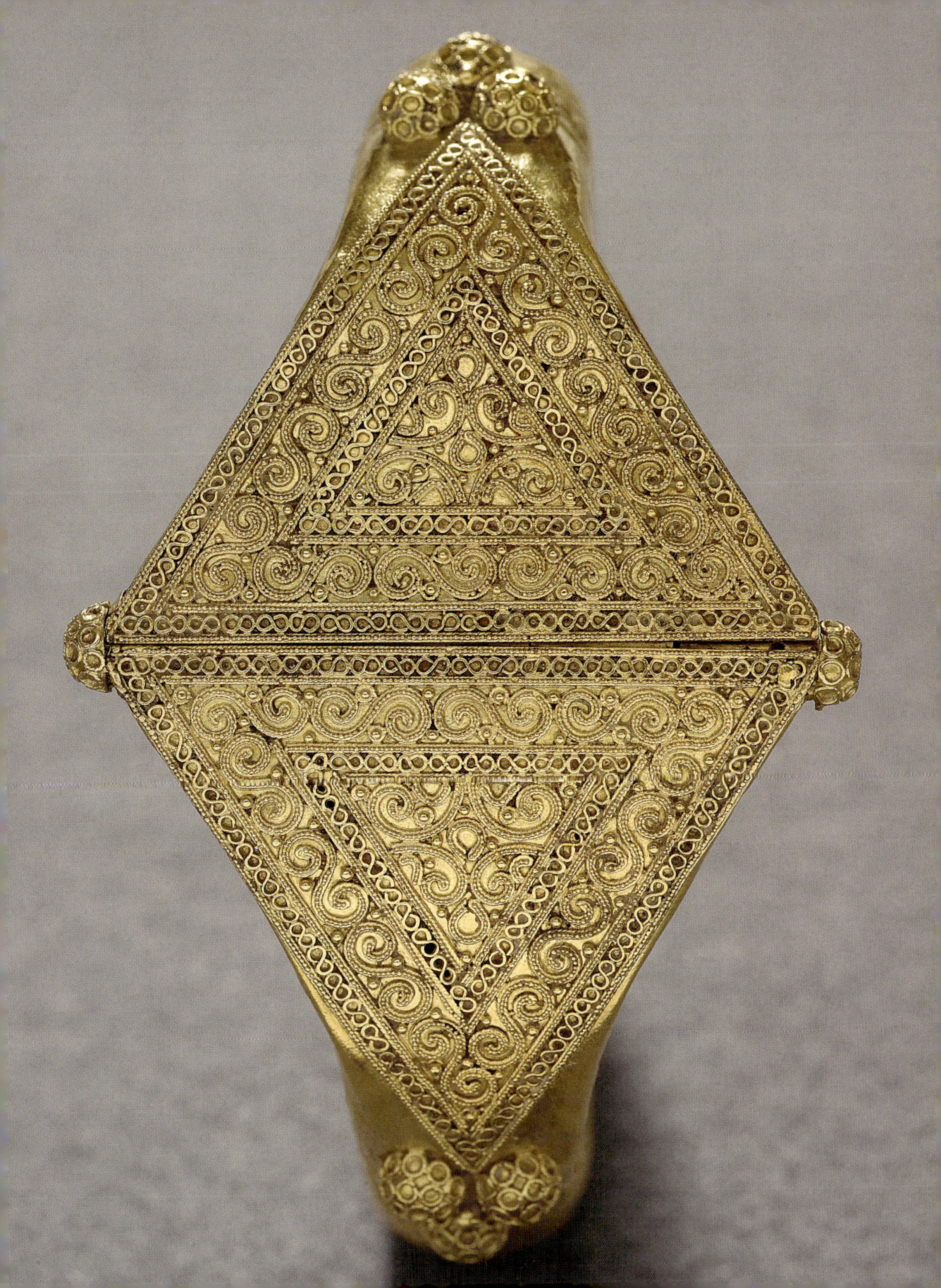

## NECKLACE

ORIGIN
India

DATE
17th century

MATERIAL
Gold, engraved spinels (Balas rubies) diamonds, pearls

DIMENSIONS
L 38.5 cm

NUMBER
JE.26.1997

49 Three of the eleven spinel beads on this necklace are engraved with the names of Jahangir and Shah Jahan, the two greatest Mughal emperors of India in the seventeenth century. Bright pinkish red spinels are known as 'Balas' rubies, named after the region of Badakhshan, in Afghanistan, where they were first reportedly mined. The Mughals had a passion for spinels which they collected in large quantities and used in much of their luxurious jewellery and turban ornaments. The gems are polished, not cut, and the emperors and other owners would have their names engraved on the flat facets of particularly prized examples.

**50** The *haldili* is a type of pendant worn to help cure the wearer of heart 'palpitations'. This *haldili* belonged to Shah Jahan and was an intimate and private amulet to help him, heartbroken, with his grief over the loss of his beloved wife, the Empress Mumtaz Mahal, who had died in 1631. He would have worn this amulet next to his heart whilst he was building the world's most famous public monument of a man's love for his wife – the Taj Mahal.

**CALLIGRAPHIC JADE PENDANT (HALDILI)**

ORIGIN
India

DATE
Dated AH 1041 [1631–32]

MATERIAL
Jade (nephrite), carved

DIMENSIONS
H 3.3 cm; L 5.1 cm

NUMBER
JE.85.2002

**EMERALD**

ORIGIN
India

DATE
Dated AH 1107 [1695–96]

MATERIAL
Emerald, carved

DIMENSIONS
H 5.1 cm; W 4 cm

NUMBER
JE.86.2002

51 Large and fine emeralds, recently brought over by European traders from Columbia, South America, found a ready and eager market among the Mughal elite. Carved emeralds were worn as a talisman with the inscription facing inwards against the skin on the upper arm. It was believed that the carving of inscriptions heightened the potency of the emerald and helped to ward off demons, as well as to prevent illness. The inscription on this magnificent emerald contains a Shi'a prayer, and probably belonged to one of the emperors' officers or noblemen, many of whom were of Shi'a Deccani or Persian origin.

52 A truly extraordinary and impressive object, this falcon is made of gold and enamel, and profusely inlaid with precious gemstones: rubies, diamonds, and emeralds. This piece was made in the Imperial Mughal workshop and was part of the private jewels of Shah Jahan. The symbolism of a falcon demonstrates kingship, whilst birds in connection with Muslim rulers represent victory and power. The falcon was a favourite symbol of the Sufi poet Rumi, who often spoke of the soul as a falcon. This bird probably decorated a throne, or was carried on a staff in formal court processions.

## JEWELLED FALCON

ORIGIN
India

DATE
c. 1640

MATERIAL
Gold with enamel and inlaid rubies, emeralds, diamonds, sapphires and onyx

DIMENSIONS
H 23.4 cm; Ø 8.3 cm; W 6.9 cm

NUMBER
JE.69.2001

# GLASS

Glass – formed essentially of heat and sand – is the child of the Middle East: it was invented there and subsequently developed there into its most sophisticated forms. Glass first arrived as a luxury in ancient Egypt and Mesopotamia. Under the Romans it was developed into an everyday material for everything from industrial containers to the most refined, expensive perfume flasks.

The Islamic world inherited this legacy: materials and skills developed to serve the needs of the burgeoning cities.

Glass is an astonishingly versatile material. It can be made cheaply as clean, capacious and convenient containers for manufacturing, storage and transport. It can be treated as a semi-precious stone. It can be manipulated into almost any shape, and decorated in a bewildering variety of techniques: hot-worked, mould-blown, incised, wheel-cut, lustre-painted, enamelled...

Almost every technique known for the decoration of glass anywhere in the world had been developed by Islamic glassworkers by the medieval period: only in the nineteenth century during the industrial revolution in Europe do we see anything new. Some age-old techniques – hot-working, mould-blowing, cutting – were taken to new heights by Islamic glassmakers. Invented or rediscovered by them was painted decoration – in particular enamelled glass, the great glory of the medieval period.

China and the Far East never developed a significant glass industry, instead importing Islamic glass as great luxuries. Fine European glass owes its origin to the Islamic world, whose secrets were adopted first in Italy, and then throughout the continent.

**BEAKER**

ORIGIN
Iraq or Egypt

DATE
9th–10th century

MATERIAL
Glass, wheel-cut

DIMENSIONS
H 8.5 cm; Ø 10 cm

NUMBER
GL.19.1999

53 The 'bevelled' style seen on this beaker was first developed in Samarra (Iraq), where it was used for the stucco decoration of the city's architecture. The style became popular around the Islamic world, migrating to Tulunid Egypt, where its design was incorporated into objects made from various materials such as glass, wood and rock crystal. This particular example is recognized as one of the most perfect examples of this style in glass, where the bevelled cuts were made by holding the glass against a revolving stone or copper wheel.

**THE 'CAVOUR' VASE**

ORIGIN
Probably Syria

DATE
Late 13th century

MATERIAL
Glass, decorated with vitreous enamel and gilding

DIMENSIONS
H 29 cm; Ø 19.7 cm

NUMBER
GL.6.1998

54 Fewer than twenty intact enamelled cobalt blue or dark purple glass objects from the Ayyubid and Mamluk dynasties exist and this is one of the premier pieces. It is particularly unusual as it is a secular object whereas mosque lamps survive more commonly. Secular objects were more at risk of damage as they were continually handled and cleaned, and when damaged were thrown away. A painted line of white Kufic against a colourful background scroll and gilded line in cursive script run around the neck of the vase. They list many titles of the unnamed patron including "Our Lord the Sultan, the ruler".

55 Made during the Mamluk period in Egypt and Syria, blown, enamelled and gilded glass oil lamps were suspended from the ceiling to illuminate buildings. Large quantities were produced in Cairo in the fourteenth century in order to decorate the profusion of mosques and tombs which the Mamluk rulers and their courtiers built with great enthusiasm. They provided decoration more than light, for which other types of oil lamp were used. Many enamelled lamps therefore hung quietly and undisturbed over centuries, until their artistic worth was recognized and they were removed from their original locations – often monuments in complete disrepair – to the safety of museums.

**MOSQUE LAMP**

ORIGIN
Egypt (Cairo)

DATE
c. 1412–15

MATERIAL
Glass, vitreous enamel, gilding

DIMENSIONS
H 28.5 cm; Ø 24.2 cm

NUMBER
GL.321.2002

# IVORY

True elephant ivory has been a luxury since very ancient times. Its material qualities were always highly valued: pearly white but taking colour easily, with a wonderful sheen when polished, and easily carved in fine detail. It was used on its own to fabricate small boxes and implements, or as a decorative inlay contrasted with black ebony. Ivory is also rare, and has never been in ample supply.

Traded north from sub-Saharan Africa, ivory was eagerly sought by successive Middle Eastern and Mediterranean cultures: ancient Egypt and Mesopotamia, classical Greece and Rome, the later Byzantines and Sasanians. The Muslims inherited this legacy, and continued the various traditions of working it.

The three items illustrated here show the most extravagant use of the material. All are made from solid pieces cut whole from the tusk: cheaper work might use thin cut sheets, bent and joined.

The chess piece – solid, heavy and plain – impresses by the material alone. Imagine the effect of the complete chess board: enormous in size with sixteen white pieces, and sixteen more in ebony or black-coloured ivory.

The Spanish box, solid with the interior hollowed out: a wasteful technique, but which gives the piece its luxurious weight. The detailed carving well demonstrates the ivory's fine-grained nature.

The oliphant proclaims its expense by its very shape – a whole natural tusk.

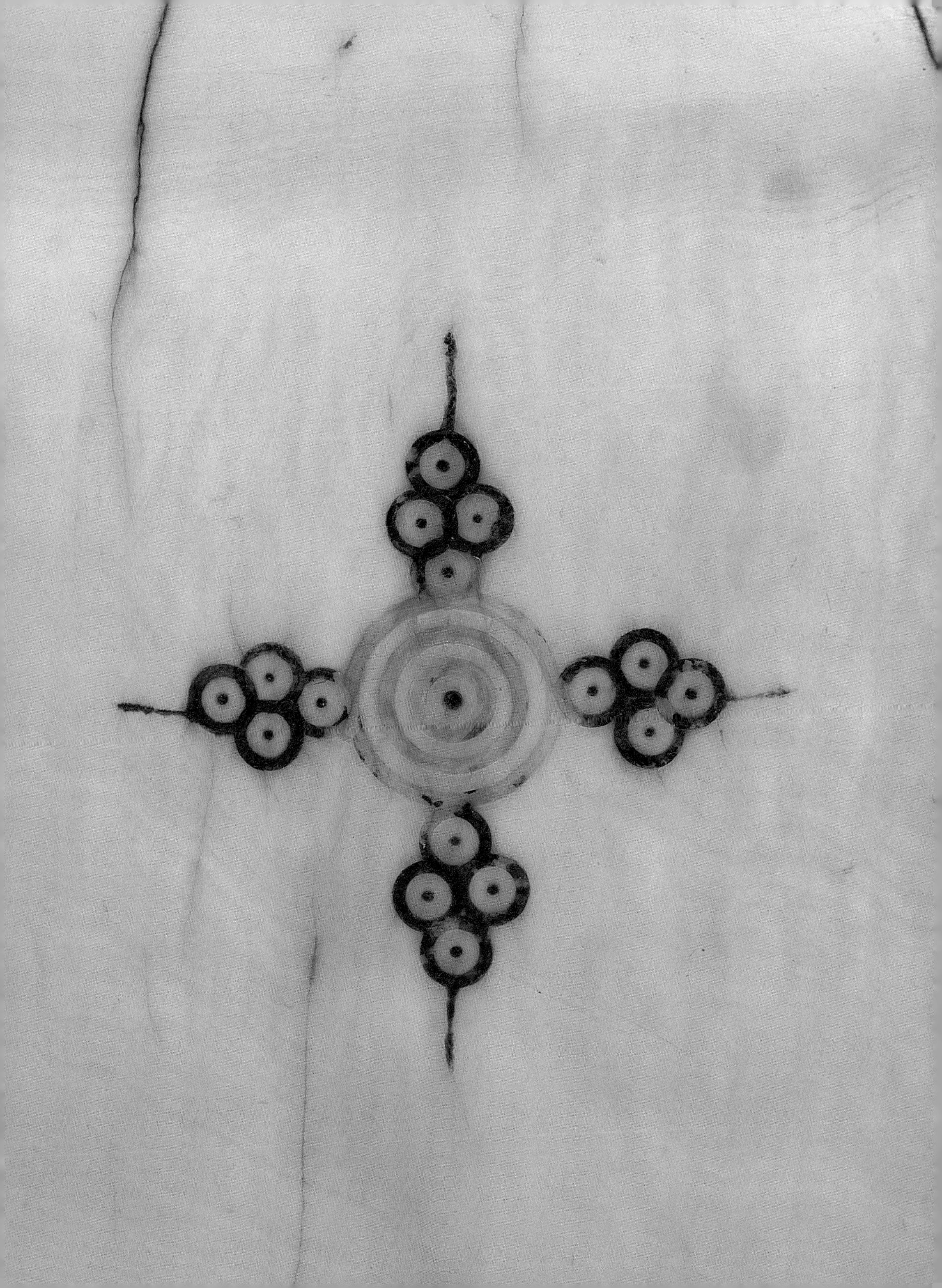

## CHESS PIECE

ORIGIN
Egypt or Sicily

DATE
11th century

MATERIAL
Ivory, coloured inlay

DIMENSIONS
H 8.5 cm; weight 610 g

NUMBER
IV.5.1998

**56** Chess was a popular indoor game and quickly spread from India throughout the Islamic world. At this time chess was played exclusively in royal and noble circles and as a consequence the pieces were often crafted from rare and expensive materials like ivory. This piece represents the *fil* – elephant – which in Europe became a bishop. We see an abstract representation of an elephant, with two short tusks. It comes from what must have been an enormous, and enormously expensive, set.

57 Unlike many other carved ivory boxes from Umayyad Spain which bear dedications to the royal family or highly placed members of the court, this box was made for an anonymous patron. However, the decoration follows exactly that of the royal boxes – with scenes of mounted huntsmen and their prey, lions wreaking revenge on the huntsmen, and the occasional mythical griffin.

The box has been well used over the centuries, with a black surface, applied after some time, which gives it the appearance of ebony rather than the white ivory of which it is actually made.

**BOX**

ORIGIN
Spain

DATE
Dated AH 394 [1003]

MATERIAL
Ivory, carved in relief, with black stain

DIMENSIONS
H 4.3; Ø 7.1 cm; L 36.7 cm

NUMBER
IV.4.1998

**OLIPHANT (HUNTING HORN)**

ORIGIN
Italy (probably Sicily)

DATE
11th–12th century

MATERIAL
Carved ivory and brass

DIMENSIONS
L 49 cm; weight 1505 g

NUMBER
IV.7.1999

58 This is essentially a European object following the Islamic aesthetic which was much admired by the Normans in Sicily at the time. Made from a single piece of elephant tusk and probably in an Italian workshop that employed Muslim artisans, these horns were highly prized and desirable objects used for communication during the hunt.

This publication was made possible by the Qatar Museums Authority.
With special thanks to Her Excellency Sheikha Al Mayassa bint Hamad bin Khalifa Al Thani, Chairperson, Qatar Museums Authority.

**Qatar Museums Authority**
CEO
Abdulla Al Najjar

**Museum of Islamic Art, Doha**
Director
Oliver Watson

Photography Coordinator
Nicolas Ferrando



Photo Credits:
Nicolas Ferrando: pages 92, 94-5, 96, 97, 105, 106, 114, 115, 118, 119, 130, 131, 138, 139, 154, 155, 156, 157, 158, 159, 160, 161 and 169
Hughes Dubois, Paris-Brussels: pages 92, 128
All other images by Lois Lammerhuber, Baden

**Prestel Verlag**
Königinstrasse 9
80539 Munich
Tel. +49 (0)89 24 29 08-300
Fax +49 (0)89 24 29 08-335

**Prestel Publishing Ltd**
4 Bloomsbury Place
London WC1A 2QA
Tel. +44 (0)20 7323-5004
Fax +44 (0)20 7636-8004

**Prestel Publishing**
900 Broadway, Suite 603
New York, N.Y. 10003
Tel. +1 (212) 995-2720
Fax +1 (212) 995-2733

www.prestel.com

Prestel books are available worldwide. Please contact your nearest bookseller or one of the above addresses for information concerning your local distributor.

The Library of Congress Cataloguing-in-Publication data is available. British Library Cataloguing-in-Publication Data: a catalogue record for this book is available from the British Library. The Deutsche Bibliothek holds a record of this publication in the Deutsche Nationalbibliografie; detailed bibliographical data can be found under: http://dnb.ddb.de.

Editorial Direction by Victoria Salley, Anja Paquin
Copy-editing by Harriet Graham, Jane Michael
Design by SOFAROBOTNIK, Augsburg and Munich
Layout by Fotosatz Huber, Germering
Design Coordination by Cilly Klotz
Production by Sebastian Runow
Pre-press production by Prepress Lammerhuber, Baden
Postproduction by Martin Ackerl, Birgit Hofbauer
Printing and Binding by TBB, Banská Bystrica
Printed on acid-free paper.

ISBN 978-3-7913-3935-1 (English edition)
ISBN 978-3-7913-3934-4 (Arabic edition)